KURDISTAN

A NATION EMERGES

KURDISTAN

A NATION EMERGES

JONATHAN FRYER

AND OTHERS

STACEY
INTERNATIONAL

KURDISTAN
first published by Stacey International in 2010

Stacey International
128 Kensington Church Street
London W8 4BH
Telephone: +44 (0)20 7221 7166
Fax: +44 (0)20 7792 9288
Email: info@stacey-international.co.uk
Website: www.stacey-international.co.uk

The publishers would like to thank the Kurdistan Regional Government for their assistance in the creation of this book, in particular Talar Faiq Salih without whose major support and contribution, this book would not have been possible.

Principal text contributions
Jonathan Fryer, Michael Howard, Parwez Zabihi, Max Scott

Editorial
Max Scott

Design
Graham Edwards

Cartography
Amber Shears

Photographic credits
The publishers would like to acknowledge the following photographers and photographic agencies for the use of their images in this book:

John Wrefford: 2/3, 6, 8/9, 11(t,m,b), 12, 13(all), 14, 15(all), 16, 17(all), 18/19(all), 20(all), 21(b), 22(t&b), 23, 24(t,m,b), 25, 26, 27(t&b), 28(t&b), 29, 30, 31, 32, 33, 34/35, 38(t&b), 39, 40, 41(t&b), 42(all), 43(all), 44, 45, 46, 47, 48(t&b), 49, 50, 51(all), 52/53, 54(l&r), 55(l&r), 56, 57(all), 58/59, 60, 62, 63, 64(t&b), 65, 66, 67, 74, 75(all), 78(l), 80, 81(all), 86, 89, 94, 95, 96(t), 97, 100, 102-103, 105, 108, 109, 112(r), 115(t&b), 118, 119, 128, 129, 132, 143, 144, 145(l&r), 146(t), 147, 149, 150, 161, The Library if the University of Texas: 10(t), 91, 92; James Gordon: 10(b); Safin Hamad: (21t), 68(l&r), 70, 71(t&b), 79, 82(t&b), 83(b), 85, 140, 146(b); Kamaran Najm/Metrography: 69, 157; Stafford Clarry: 72(t&b), 73; TAW Photographic Agency: 36/37, 78(r), 83(t), 148(l); Kurdistan in the Shadow of History: 90(t), 90(b), 93, 96(b); Corbis: 98, 99; Photos: 84, 101(l&r), 106, 130, 131, 134, 138(l&r), 139(t&b), 153, 156, 155, 158; Ghetty Images: 110, 116, 114, 120, 122, 123, 124, 125, 126, 127, 135; Talar Faiq: 112(l), The KRG Department of Foreign Relations: 121(b), 136, 137, 141, 152, 154; Golden Screen Films: 113(r); Alamy: front jacket.

ISBN: 978 1 906 768188

CIP Data: A catalogue record for this book is available from the British Library

Printed in China

Title page:
A solitary angler fishes in the tranquil waters of Lake Dokan.

Map of the provinces inside the Kurdish Regional Government area of Iraq

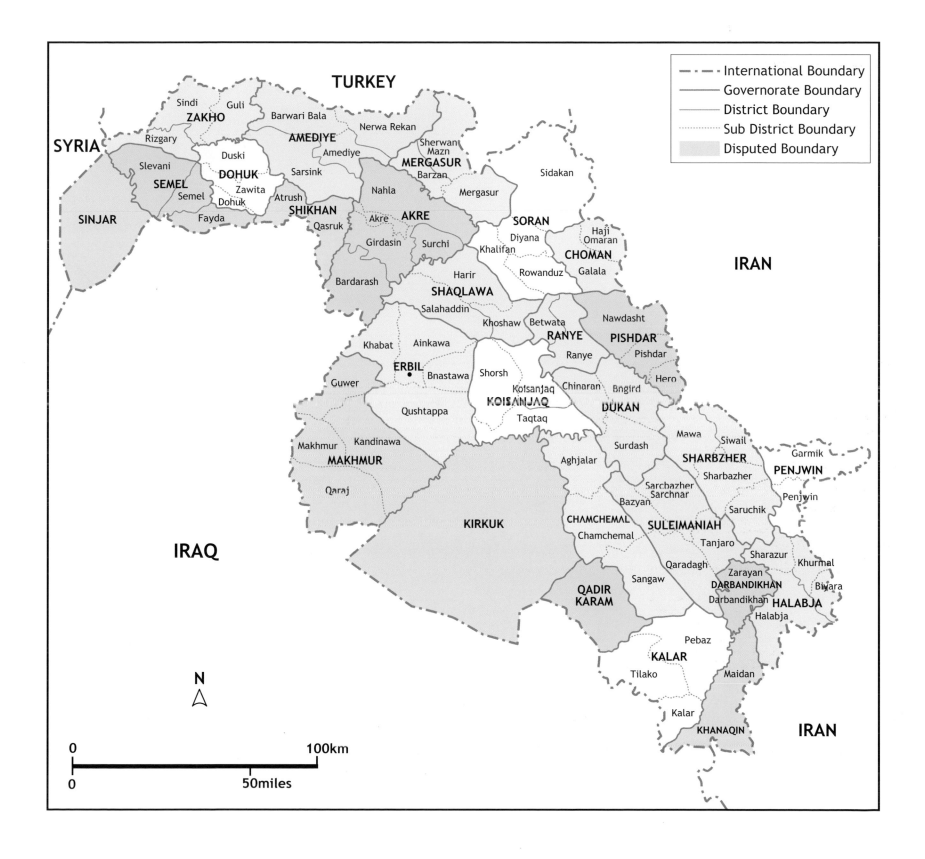

Legend:
- International Boundary
- Governorate Boundary
- District Boundary
- Sub District Boundary
- Disputed Boundary

TURKEY

SYRIA

IRAN

IRAQ

IRAN

Sindi · Guli · ZAKHO · Barwari Bala · Nerwa Rekan
Rizgary · AMEDIYE · Amediye · Sherwan Mazn · MERGASUR · Sidakan
Duski · DOHUK · Sarsink · Barzan
Slevani · Zawita · Atrush · SHIKHAN · Nahla · Mergasur
SEMEL · Semel · Dohuk · AKRE · SORAN
SINJAR · Fayda · Qasruk · Akre · Diyana · Haji Omaran
Girdasin · Surchi · Khalifan · CHOMAN
Bardarash · Harir · Rowanduz · Galala
SHAQLAWA
Salahaddin
Khoshaw · Betwata · Nawdasht
Khabat · Ainkawa · RANYE · PISHDAR
ERBIL · Bnastawa · Shorsh · Ranye · Pishdar
Guwer · Kotsanjaq · Chinaran · Bngird · Hero
Qushtappa · KOISANJAQ · DUKAN
Taqtaq · Mawa · Siwail
Makhmur · Kandinawa · Surdash · SHARBZHER · Garmik
MAKHMUR · Aghjalar · Sharbazher · PENJWIN
Qaraj · Sarcbazher · Sarchnar · Penjwin
Bazyan · Saruchik
KIRKUK · CHAMCHEMAL · SULEIMANIAH
Chamchemal · Tanjaro
Qaradagh · Sharazur · Khurmal
Sangaw · Zarayan · DARBANDIKHAN
QADIR KARAM · Darbandikhan · HALABJA · Biyara
Halabja
Pebaz
KALAR
Tilako · Maidan
Kalar
KHANAQIN

N

0 ___ 100km
0 ___ 50miles

Contents

1

LAND &
PEOPLE

Erbil lies on the plain beneath the mountains, but, for the most part, the inhabitants of Iraqi Kurdistan dwell up above in the rugged and rocky terrain that is the traditional habitat of the Kurds since time immemorial.

With peace now established, an era may now be emerging that will see the sons and daughters of Zuhak starting to come back down to the fertile lowlands and build settled and prosperous lives there. But in the Kurdish spirit the atavistic yearning for their ancient mountain fastness is never like to fade completely.

The iconic statue of the ancient Kurdish historian Ibn Mustafi stands by the entranceway to the citadel and its ancient raised dwellings in the centre of Erbil, capital to modern day Kurdistan.

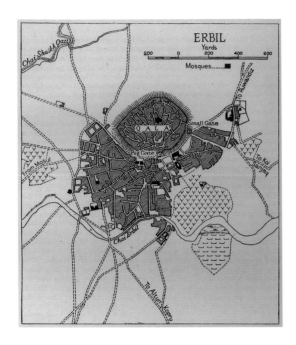

The citadel, thought to be built upon an early tell, stands on a man-made plateau some 26 metres above the surrounding plain (***below right***). The main front gate can be clearly seen to the fore. It is within these fortified walls that Erbil's citizens have traditionally lived. The bazaars spread out and downwards to the south-west (map of Erbil from 1954 ***above***).

Erbil

Erbil – the name most used internationally for the ancient city that serves as today's capital of Iraqi Kurdistan – is often referred to by the phonetic equivalents of Arbil or Erbil, as well as Arbela. The origin of the name can be traced back to Sumerian writings as early as 2000 BC referring to Arbilum, Orbelum or Urbilum. It is believed to be composed from the Sumerian roots 'Ur' (town) and 'Bela' (high), presumably on the basis that it is located in the upper regions, beyond the lower deltas of the Tigris. In the Kurdish language the city is still referred to as Hawler, linked perhaps to the Greek *helios* (sun) and denoting a sun temple, in recognition of the early Zoroastrian worship of fire and sun.

There are traces of early settled existence in the Erbil region as far back as the twenty-third century BC, but probably the first major population expansion took place when Cyaxares (625 – 585 BC), the first king of Media, settled some of the sagarthian tribes in what is today Erbil and Kirkuk. Neighbours to the Parthians in north eastern Iran, these early Persian tribes were nomadic pastoralists, reputed to use the lasso as their principal weapon. The Medes, and with them the Sagarthians, were to revolt against Darius I of Persia in 522 BC, but this revolt was firmly put down by the army which Darius sent out under the leadership of General Takhmaspada the following year. The events are depicted in the Behistun Inscription which stands today in the mountains of Iran's Kermanshah province.

Ever the buffer zone between the two great empires of Byzantium and Persia, the plains 10km to the west of Erbil were to witness the Battle of Gaugemela between Alexander the Great and Darius III of Persia in 331 BC. Vanquished, Darius managed to flee to Erbil, which is why the battle is still sometimes referred to – rather inaccurately – as the Battle of Erbil.

Erbil went on to be the seat of rule for the Adiabene Kingdom in the first century AD, largely located to the north west in the region of modern day Diyarbakir in Turkey. It is remembered in Jewish traditions for the notable conversion of its Queen, Helena of Adiabene, to Judaism before she moved on to Jerusalem. Early Christianity was also to flourish in Erbil with a bishop established in the town as early as AD 100 with a community of followers thought to be converts from Judaism.

The main gate is guarded by an immense statue of a Kurd reading (***bottom***). The houses of the citadel behind him are built into the stony ground of the mound (***middle***) and look down on the streets and tarmacked roads that circle them (***right***).

TEXTILES

Kurdistan has a long and distinguished history of textile-making and its weavers are famous throughout the region for the high quality and unique designs of their crafts. The most famous Kurdish textile product is the carpet, and Kurdish carpet designs are imitated and popular all over the Middle East. This is particularly so in Iran, in the major rug-producing towns of Hamadan, Arak and elsewhere in Lorestan, where for centuries Kurdish carpets have had a strong influence on the design and style of Persian carpets.

Many nomadic Kurdish communities are accustomed to using a barter system rather than money (even today) and this has helped to ensure that the materials in Kurdish rugs and textiles are genuine and of the highest quality. Pure wool is used in preference to artificial fibres, and there is a ready supply of such materials from the sheep and goats that nomads keep with them in their villages or mobile camps. Natural vegetable colours are extracted from wild plants and used to make dyes. Undyed wool is also widely used and is derived from the natural wool colours of animals, such as ivory, grey and brown. This includes white wool, which is collected in spring when the animals' wool is lightest in tint .

A number of different textiles are manufactured in Kurdistan. The most widely produced is the kilim, a flat tapestry-woven rug, used both as decoration and functionally as a prayer rug. There is also the *jajim*, a multi-purpose textile that can be made in different degrees of thickness and size, and in different forms, such as bedclothes, blankets and furniture coverings. There are also more specialised textile products such as sitting mats and bread-making mats which are made from felt.

Kurdish carpets are known for their robust, heavy quality, and are extremely durable and solid. They usually consist of a woollen foundation with cotton warps and wefts woven on top of this. Sometimes a kilim can incorporate both a woven and an embroidered pattern in the same piece. Kurdish weaving patterns and motifs tend to consist of either geometrical patterns or floral designs. The weaver will rarely plan the overall layout beforehand, instead preferring to let the design develop gradually as the carpet is produced. Each carpet reflects the aptitude, taste and birthplace of the maker and it is rare to find perfect symmetry or consistency of pattern in Kurdish rugs.

Today, the art of carpet weaving and other textile manufacturing is under threat, mainly because nomadic communities are dwindling and factory-made products are on the increase. However, attention is being devoted to preserving this important tradition. The Kurdish Textile Museum opened in Erbil in 2004, displaying carpets and traditional Kurdish clothes and hats – see *opposite*. The museum promotes the continued hand-production of textiles and ensures that the skills and knowledge of the older generation of weavers is passed on to the younger generation.

For a long period the region was to fall under the thrall of Roman power, with the Sassanians attempting forays into the region at intervals. Under Emperor Trajan it was declared the Roman Province of Assyria in AD 116, although the naming does not seem to have outlived his rule. The Emperor Jovian was to abandon the region in AD 363, withdrawing to Constantinople to consolidate his rule, leaving a peace agreement in place with the Sassanians.

The Kurdish and Aramaic-speaking Assyrian communities continued to flourish across the region, alongside Arab populations, with skirmishes occurring at intervals, until the arrival of Tamerlane (Timur) at the start of the fifteenth Century. Tamerlane laid waste to most of what he came across, reputedly leaving only one Christian village standing. Erbil was, from then onwards, to become dominated by its increasing Muslim population, with converts from the various ethnic communities – be they Turkic, Persian, Arab or Kurdish – finding life easier once they had embraced Islam.

From this time forward, the city of Baghdad grew to be the regional hub, a base for a succession of empires who were to rule Erbil as a province: the Abbasids through to the Ottomans in the nineteenth century. It was the Ottomans who were to build the fort atop the ancient tell that stands in the centre of modern Erbil. The city grew beyond its original walls and established itself as a significant trading centre on the route between Mosul and Baghdad.

As capital of Kurdish Iraq, the city played a central role in the development of the Kurdish movement for recognition and autonomy, suffering ransack by the forces of Saddam Hussein in the 1990s, but enjoying the benefits of economic growth as the autonomous region of Kurdistan took shape. The population has grown to four or five times its size in 1992 with ecomomic migrants being drawn in from the various outlying villages surrounding the city.

As we fly into the centre of the Kurdistan Region of Iraq today, into an airport that was

(continues on page 20)

The Jalil Khayat Mosque of Erbil was recently completed (*above*) and its fine ornamentation (*below and opposite*) showcases the arts of craftsmen from across the world

THE CITADEL AND THE BAZAAR

In common with other trading centres in the region, gold is sold by weight (*left*), a major commodity whose price is keenly monitored and of which every household holds a small store. The ancient covered bazaar in Erbil houses traders clustered by their specialisms, be they tin pots, rafia hangings or wooden cots (*opposite*).

Overleaf:

Today, the 500 or so dwellings atop Erbil's central mound stand almost all empty, a great many of them succumbing with speed to the attrition of the elements. It is hard to imagine how a new community can be re-established here once these houses have been restored and it seems increasingly likely that, with Erbil's increasing influx of tourists from across the region, a number of these streets will be developed into a communal leisure and market area.

The city of Erbil is defined by the central circular mound that is the citadel, 102,000 square metres of land raised 26 metres above the surrounding city, presumed to have been started in antiquity as a tell. Around and beneath it to the south sprawl a maze of alleyways where the ancient commercial heart of the city beats strongly to this day.

The citadel dwellings still stand, although they are now vacated as part of the UNESCO development project to renovate the buildings. Former resident Mahmoud Yasim, who grew up with his seven siblings in the 8,000-year-old network of alleyways alongside some 830 other families, describes the community they enjoyed: 'Everyone used to know each other back then. We were living in houses without permission and they were very old and part collapsed – but our life was good. We were close to everything – the bazaar, the hospital and schools as well.' A great many of the inhabitants were sad to leave when the authorities relocated them in 1997 – largely to Qalai Nwe (the 'New Citadel') – but it has afforded the opportunity to start work on rebuilding the crumbling structures, restoring wherever possible the intricate plasterwork and distinctively carved lintels.

William Hay, in his book *Two Years in Kurdistan 1918 – 1920,* reports the scene as described to him then by the English governor of the city:

> Erbil, with its battlemented heights and its great solitary minaret presents an unique appearance. The upper town, built on a huge circular mound commands the surrounding plain like a vast fort, the outer walls being lofty and containing only small irregular windows like loopholes, except where some of the rich *aghas* have constructed balconies … the streets within are very rough and narrow, and cannot be used for wheeled traffic … the lower town clusters round the south and east sides of the mound, here is the bazaar.

The market area below is thought to have been created in the time of Sultan Muzafferddin Kokberi (1190-1233). This period, the only time in its long history when Erbil flourished as an independent city state, also saw the creation of the minaret recently restored in downtown Erbil, and was also the time when the Muzafferddin madrassahs (schools) were founded.

The area around the southern base of the citadel has received the attention of modern town planners, with the large open-air Lana market where once market stalls sold leather crafts now razed and replaced by a large modern shopping mall. The covered market, known as the Qasariyah, still stands largely unchanged: a labyrinth of small alleyways protected from sun and rain by a latticework of corrugated iron. Beneath these eaves are the numerous shopkeepers selling wares largely imported from the Far East interspersed with craftsmen plying a trade they would have inherited from their forefathers in the late nineteenth century when the bazaar was restored: jewellers, cobblers, carpenters, tinsmiths and butchers. Where possible, tradesmen gather alongside others who trade in the same wares, giving each alleyway a specialism such as the passageway towards the north-east corner where honey and dairy products are sold – yoghurts and cheeses piling high onto shelves already crowded with jars of the highly valued local honey. Another highly prized tradition is the creation of Klash shoes – an ancient uniquely Kurdish craft when white cloth is beaten on small anvils to create hard-wearing footwear. These, and the traditional fabrics sold in the textile souk, are ever-popular in the run-up to the annual Newroz celebrations when the townspeople assume traditional attire.

Not far from the crumbling structures of the citadel lie the recent developments which form the new town of Erbil. Shown here are: Majidi Mall (*opposite top*), a major new shopping centre unlike anything previously in the capital; the English Village (*above and above right*) where modern houses are built in a walled community, a project mirrored in the American Village and the Italian Village, amongst others; the Sami Abdul Rahman Park, a rolling expanse of grass and trees where the town's inhabitants take their rest, go boating (*right*) or bring their children to play (*opposite bottom*).

created as recently as 2004, with the new sister airport opened only in 2010 and boasting some of the highest design, engineering and safety specifcations in the world, we are welcomed by a region that has been radically transformed but is still only at the beginning of its development. Erbil's change has been fast, and dramatic. Where the largest military base in northern Iraq

once stood, a huge area opposite the Iraqi Kurdistan Parliament (IKP) is today a fresh and dramatic demonstration of rebirth. The area includes a major nature park with rose gardens, waterways, playgrounds and a climbing wall. Within the same former military area are international trade-fair facilities, luxury hotels, gated communities of modern homes

under construction, a modern library, amusement areas including a go-cart speedway, modern shopping malls and a conference centre that would be the pride of any city anywhere in the world. A new airport with the fifth longest public runway in the world opened in 2010. Longer runways are necessary to take the largest and heaviest planes on the hottest days when temperatures exceed fifty degrees Celsius and the air is 'thin' and lighter.

Since 2003, old streets have been widened and new streets have been constructed throughout the city. Overpasses and underpasses have been completed along with new amusement parks, including an aqua park, bowling alleys and an ice rink. Many thousands of new and renovated homes are completed and occupied. Thousands of more homes are in progress. New businesses, including shopping areas with hundreds of stores, airline offices and travel agents, have opened. Almost every kind of new vehicle is available and so are most luxury items.

More importantly, since 2003, new and modern schools and universities have opened in Erbil. Over half the Kurdistan Region's nearly five million population is under twenty years of age. Throughout the Region, more than 1.2 million children attend some 5,000 primary and secondary schools to learn from over 70,000 teachers. By raising educational standards, education quality is being addressed within the government school system and by an increasing number of new private schools and universities. Education is not only conducted in Kurdish, but also in English, a language that is being emphasised from the earliest grades. For students whose mother language is Arabic, Syriac or Turkmani, there are schools fully funded by the KRG that teach in these languages – nowhere else in Iraq are government-funded schools teaching in so many languages.

One of the oldest and largest institutions of higher learning in the Kurdistan Region is Salahaddin University, established in 1968 and originally based in Suleimaniah. It transferred to Erbil in 1981. Initially, the university

included seven colleges: Science, Agriculture, Engineering Administration, Arts, Education, and Medicine. Later, in 1985, the College of Law and Politics was added to the University's programmes while the College of Dentistry was added in 1995.

The total number of colleges became 22 in 2004 and then decreased to 18 in 2005 when

the Colleges of Medicine, Dentistry, Nursing, and Pharmacy became part of the separate Hawler Medical University.

Another significant tertiary level educational institution in Erbil is The BMU – the Lebanese French University or Business and Management University, a newly established and offering programs at Bachelor's and Master's levels

At the main entrance to the administration buildings of Salahaddin University stands the imposing statue of one of the University's first chancellors (*right*), flanked now on warm days by students taking the sun on the grass. The university, as the main seat of learning in Erbil, will draw students from a broad range of ages and backgrounds taught increasingly by Kurdish academics who are returning to their homeland to have a stake in the country's future – a reversal of the brain drain that happened in Saddam Hussein's times.

in Business Administration, Public Administration, Administration & Law, Economics and Information Technology. BMU has signed partnership agreements with University of Picardie Jules Verne (UPJV), Jean Moulin University Lyon 3 and Université du Québec à Chicoutimi (UQAC).

The other major centre for students in Erbil is the University of Koya, whose foundation stone was laid in 2003 by Jalal Talabani, the Iraqi president, paving the way for six colleges: Engineering, Agriculture, Science, Law, Arts and Education.

Today, Erbil's population has risen above the one million mark and looks set for further swift growth, with the administration working hard to ensure the infrastructure that will enable continued growth at the same rate.

Choueifat School is the largest private school in the Middle East. With a curriculum based upon the European system and taught in English, the school has a staff of some ten different nationalities teaching over 1,000 children between the ages of three and fourteen.

The road from Erbil up into the mountains of the northwest rises following the river (*left*). For all the aridity of the mountain peaks in the hotter months, water flows freely in most clefts, bridged frequently by military pontoons (from which the image *above* is shot), the legacy of Saddam Hussein's attempts to provide his troops better access.

It would be fair to say that the great centres of civilisation throughout the ages have tended to centre themselves further downstream from regions inhabited by the Kurds. The mountains above Erbil's plain have seen the vanguards and rearguards of great armies passing through them, and the residents have variously been affected by the rise and fall of empires in the lowlands beneath them, but this same terrain that provided the Kurds with shelter and a degree of independence also made it an inhospitable location for great urban centres. Today, roads to the most inaccessible eerie locations are good – an ironically positive result of Saddam Hussein's efforts to make the region accessible to his troops – and modern communications bring the village dwellers closer to day-to-day events in the wider world.

The resources of these mountains were drawn upon by the lowland centres since

ancient times: not only the able minds and bodies of the Kurds providing an influx of fresh manpower for infrastructure projects, but also the mountain water which was badly needed for wider agriculture projects on the plains. It was probably Sennacherib, fearsome ruler of the Assyrian Kingdom from 704 to 681 BC, who first directed energy to channelling water southwards to the magnificent city of Nineveh and its outlying agricultural lands. An elaborate system of eighteen aqueducts was constructed, and, remarkably, remains can be found today, most noticeably at Jerwana, near the modern day village of Shekhan. The carved boulders lie largely as they were conceived to stand, bridging a gap in the plain – where life-giving water once flowed to the ancient capital; today goats graze, tended by an Arab shepherd boy.

Sweeping east towards Persia, it was on the level plains near Chahra, east of Erbil, that

The shepherd here lives with his family in a small hut just off the edge of the plain. He would be unaware that the flat expanse where he grazes his sheep was the site where Darius the Great prepared unsuccessfully to defend himself against Alexander's armies in 331 BC, or that the piles of rocks around which he steers his livestock were once an aqueduct, part of Sennacherib's grand schemes to bring water down to the ancient city of Nineveh.

Alexander the Great came face to face with the forces of Darius III of Persia. The Battle of Gaugemela, also known as the Battle of Erbil, took place in 331 BC and the resulting massive victory for the Greeks was to lead to the fall of the Persian Empire.

Alexander had already enjoyed resounding military successes as he passed across the eastern Mediterranean, through Anatolia and into Syria, crossing the Euphrates and the Tigris rivers unopposed. Darius, aware of the impending threat, had pulled in men and arms from the length and breadth of the Persian empire to build a massive army – as much as 100,000 strong by some accounts – to resist the Greeks' onslaught. Mindful of his army's superior size, Darius was careful to position his forces on a flat plain that could afford his opponent no possible advantage and would allow him maximum flexibility in deploying his gigantic forces.

While there is much debate about the exact size of Darius' army, it was clearly large, and sources agree that the Persians substantially outnumbered the Greeks. Alexander's forces were, however, better trained and equipped.

The Greek Pezhetairoi – the footsoldiers who formed the backbone of the army – were armed with sarissas, six-metre spears that were longer than anything the Persians were carrying. The Persian army had a smaller core of spear-carrying infantrymen and depended largely upon bow and arrow.

On the eve of battle, Alexander resisted his generals' suggestions that they stage a surprise night attack in an attempt to give them the edge over the superior force. It turned out to be a wise course – Darius' men spent the night in watchfulness for just such an eventuality and were less well rested than the Greek force when it came to time to engage.

At dawn, Darius' forces advanced in V formation, seeking to draw the Greeks onwards. Alexander, employing a strategy rarely used in the history of battlefield tactics, brought his cavalry round the flanks and sought to draw the Persians outwards, leaving a vulnerable core open to attack.

The tactic succeeded and a large part of the Persian forces were routed, with some accounts reporting that they fled in terror, led by a despairing Darius. Alexander was keen to pursue the fallen king, but Darius' life was spared as the Greek was obliged to come to the aid of one flank of his forces which was in trouble.

The Arab population in the main Kurdish regions is small, but the shepherd family shown here (*above*) lives in a small hut on the plain that sweeps across to Chahra (*right*) and traces its lineage, through oral tradition, to ancient times.

Darius' escape was shortlived. He had managed to flee the battle alive with a small core of his forces remaining intact, but his empire was fragmented, divided now into east and west, and his authority diminished. He was soon to be murdered by one of his generals, and it was not long before Alexander was to lead his triumphant forces into Persia proper. Most historians would agree that it was this battle that signalled the end of the Persian Empire.

Dohuk (sometimes known as Dahuk or Dihok), Iraqi Kurdistan's third city, nestles in a valley in the Zagros mountains in the far north-west of the country, capital to the governorate of the same name. Since ancient times, Dohuk has been a crossroads for the various armies of Byzantium and Persia and today stands at the crossroads between Syria, Turkey and Iran.

Circled by mountains along the Tigris River, Dohuk is a picturesque city with a thriving tourist industry – a haven of peace for Iraqis of all nationalities from further south. None of the fighting which raged across neighbouring areas was experienced in Dohuk, and the

The older generation (**above**) and the young (**left**) gather alike on Shindoka mountain above Dohuk to enjoy the evening sun and the vista of the city below.

infrastructure consequently did not suffer the sort of damage experienced elsewhere across Iraq. The population has grown swiftly over the past two decades, reaching some two million souls today, chiefly Kurds.

Foreign investment in Dohuk continues to rise, manifested in the rising number of modern residential and office buildings as well as malls. It is known also as a cultural centre, with a thriving museum and a number of private art galleries. The University of Dohuk is one of the country's leading centres for teaching and research, centred in a building that once served as an army barracks for Saddam's soldiers. Founded with just 149 students over two colleges in 1992, the campus has now grown to thirteen colleges with more than 10,000 undergraduate students and 500 Postgraduate students.

The other major town in the governorate is Zakho, famous for the distinctively designed Delal Bridge that crosses the Little Khabour River. The main River Khabour, of which this is a tributary, flows around the town to the west, forming the border between Iraq and Turkey, and is itself a tributary of the Tigris with its mountain waters flowing down to eventually join the Euphrates before running into the

Persian Gulf. With a population today of around 500,000, Zakho is a border town, and has long served as a checkpoint for the border with Turkey.

The main road through the town carries tourists and large numbers of trucks – the chief conduit for the burgeoning trade between Kurdistan and her largest trading partner, Turkey.

The town has an ancient history. William Francis Ainsworth, passing through in 1844 commented:

> 'The appearance of Zakhu in the present day coincides in a remarkable manner with what it was described to be in the time of Xenophon.'

Gertrude Bell, the renowned British archaeologist and Arabist who advised British governors in the region in the closing years of the British Mandate, was convinced that Zakho was the same place as the ancient town of Hasaniyeh. She also reported that one of the first Christian missionaries to the region, the Dominican monk Poldo Soldini, was buried there in 1779. The town is also the site of Zakho castle, of which today only the tower remains, and of Qubad Pasha castle, a hexagonal structure in Zakho cemetery.

Following the rebellion of the Kurdish population in 1991, coordinated to support the Western military attacks of the first Gulf War, Saddam's reprisals were fierce and brutal, and large numbers of the townspeople were obliged to seek refuge up in the neighbouring mountains. Today's flourishing city has come a long way from the near ghost town described by American military forces arriving in 1991 as part of Operation Provide Comfort – a project to protect the Kurdish population from Saddam's reprisals. The American military

The distinctive Delal Bridge (*above*) is one of Kurdistan's most famous landmarks, its unusual shape mimicked in smaller bridges elsewhere across the region. Constructed from unusually large blocks of stone, the bridge was originally assembled with lifting techniques and long-lost skills baffling to today's experts.

The view from the mountain top near Dohuk (*previous spread*) looks north to Turkey – a serene valley today, but not so long ago the concourse for Turkish troops and PKK forces waging fierce guerrilla warfare.

presence was finally withdrawn in 1996, and the town suffered again as significant numbers of the better educated and better qualified professionals relocated to America, a braindrain that left a shortage of skilled manpower to regenerate the city.

In the event, the flourishing Kurdish economy following the last Gulf War was to provide ample impetus to compensate for this and drive the city's growth. Relations with Turkey improved sharply, and continue to strengthen, and Zakho, situated on the main trade route south, benefits from the flow of produce and construction materials that passes through its streets and onwards, not only to Kurdistan but also to the wider Iraqi region as a whole.

Both Dohuk and Zakho are situated on minor tributaries of the River Tigris. Further south-east, Erbil lies on a plain in the uplands between the Great and Little Zab Rivers which also flow down to join the Tigris. Thence the waters converge and sweep down to Mosul, onwards to converge with the Euphrates by Basra and then down to join the waters of the Persian Gulf. The mighty Tigris, rising in the Tauris Mountains of south-eastern Turkey, and over one thousand miles long, is fed from the east largely from Kurdish soil until it reaches the lowlands.

The Tigris is heavily dammed in Iraq and Turkey to provide water for irrigating the arid and semi-desert regions bordering the river valley. Historically, such damming has been seen as helpful in averting floods in Iraq, a frequent occurrence following the spring thaw and the melting of snow in the Turkish mountains around April, but increased damning in Turkey in recent years has prompted concerns of potential droughts in future. The dam at Mosul is the largest in Iraq.

The Great (or Upper) Zab River rises in the mountains of south-eastern Turkey and flows south for some 265 miles into Kurdistan before joining the Tigris south of the city of Mosul at the ancient biblical town of Calah. In Islamic history it is perhaps best remembered as the location of the Battle of the Zab between the Umayyads and the Abbasids.

It forms the approximate political boundary of the KRG area of Iraq today. Its sister, the Little (or Lower) Zab rises in north-western Iran, in the north of Piranshahr city and flows south-west through Iraq to join the Tigris north of the town of Baiji. The Dukan Dam straddles the Little Zab some 150 miles upstream from its confluence with the Tigris River. Constructed between 1954 and 1959, the dam

A patriotic flag has been painted on the brickwork of the dam at Dohuk (*above*). To one side of the dam lies the reclaimed land (*top*), now a popular resort and play area for children, while to the other (*right*) the gathered water lies tranquil beneath the rocky slopes from which it has descended.

Recent years have seen a sharp increase in domestic tourism, with Arab Iraqis coming north to the Kurdish areas for their beauty and security. The coachload of travellers (***below right***) will be one of many to have voyaged from as far afield as Baghdad and Basra, along well-surfaced if mountainous trails (***such as opposite***) to picnic at sites such as Sulav (***far right***) with its fresh running water and the bridge reminiscent of the well-known Delal bridge at Zakho.

has a total discharge capability of 4,300 cms. The power station, constructed in 1979, holds five water turbines and provides 400 MW of electrical energy.

The Zagros Mountains stretch a total of some 900 miles across the Iran/Iraq border. They take their name from the Zagarthians (or Sagarthians), a Kurdish people who once inhabited the mountains from the shores of Lake Van to the coasts of Makran. With a geological age similar to the Alps, they were formed by the collision of two tectonic plates – the Eurasian and Arabian Plates – a collision which is shown by recent measurements still to be active.

Stresses induced in the earth's crust by the collision caused extensive folding of the pre-existing layered sedimentary rocks. Subsequent erosion removed softer rocks, such as mudstone (rock formed by consolidated mud) and siltstone (a slightly coarser-grained mudstone), while leaving harder rocks, such as limestone (calcium-rich rock consisting of the remains of marine organisms) and dolomite (rocks similar to limestone containing calcium and magnesium). This differential erosion

formed the linear ridges of the Zagros Mountains.

The tectonic history of the rocks is conducive to the formation and trapping of petroleum, and the Zagros region is an important part of Persian Gulf oil production. Salt domes and salt glaciers are a common feature of the Zagros Mountains. Salt domes are an important target for oil exploration, as the impermeable salt frequently traps petroleum beneath other rock layers.

Average rainfall across the range is between 400 mm and 800 mm, falling mostly in the winter and spring. Winters are severe, with winter temperatures dropping as low as -25C, while the summer and autumn climate tends to be very dry.

Perched atop a small mountain, Amediye, (also known as Amadia) was, for most of its 3,000-year history, only accessible by a narrow stairway cut into the rock on the northern face. The flat plateau across the top of the mountain measures no more than 1.5 square kilometres with 1,200 dwellings crammed into the strategically safe area.

Local lore has it that the plain on which the

The town of Amediye, balanced on the small plateau of a lonely hill (*left*) has a unique defensive position, with steep sides and unbreachable city walls that allow for access through a solitary doorway (***opposite bottom, left and right***). The carvings in its archway speak of the diverse communities that dwell inside — aside from its mosques, the town houses the ruins of a synagogue and the working Church of Mary Youssef built in the 1950s.

It is perhaps its invulnerability that has led to Amediye being home to a number of notable figures in the Kurdish freedom movement. Some are celebrated in statues and paintings in the town, among them Martyr Azzat Abdulaziz, 1912 – 47 (***below right)*** who is recorded on the statue's base as one of the founder members of the KDP and Athnil Shaliman Barwani (***below left***) who died in 1961, recorded here as the first Christian Kurdish martyr.

Although there existed some sort of infrastructure for transport and communications, in the early twentieth century much of the country was inaccessible and remote, with travel difficult. Today, the landscape is criss-crossed with tarmacked roads, albeit frequently hugging tightly knitted contours of rock.

mountain town sits was home to the Magi priests of Ancient Persia, among them the most significant of Magi priests, the Three Wise Men, who made a pilgrimage to Jerusalem to see Jesus Christ shortly after his birth.

The narrow winding streets also hold relics from the Assyrian era and ruins of a synagogue and a church. The 1907 edition of the Catholic Encyclopaedia tells us that the population then already numbered 6,000, of whom 2,500 were Kurds, 1,900 Jews and 1,600 Chaldeans.

Today Amediye has a well-integrated community of Christians and Muslims that share the city and local social events.

Perched high above some of the deepest ravines and sharpest inclines of the entire Zagros range, Rowanduz stands remote and aloof from the settled plains of Erbil and Suleimaniah. Here, inaccessible to marauding armies, and fiercely independent, the mountain peoples have guarded a strong sense of independence through the ages.

Named after the Castle of Rawends (Orontes in Hellenic sources), Rowanduz was the capital of the Soran Emirate for most of its turbulent history spanning more than four hundred years. The Kingdom came under close Ottoman control in the 1530s when Suleiman the Magnificent captured Baghdad, and executed the Emir of Soran. In time, the Kingdom managed to rid itself of the Ottoman yoke, but is probably remembered most for its final ruler, Mir Mohammad. Also known as Merkor, Mir Mohammad replaced his father as the ruler of Soran in 1813 and set about ruthlessly eliminating potential opponents, including his uncles and their sons. He subdued the surrounding tribes, killing any chiefs who would not submit to his rule and establishing a reputation for particular brutality to Christians. On seeing that Mir Mohammad had seized control as far afield as Erbil, and concerned at what he might do next, the Governor of Baghdad invested him as Pasha. In 1834 the Ottomans set out to reconquer Mir Mohammad's territories. They tricked him into believing he would be reinstated by the Ottomans, but on his return he disappeared

The mountain terrain (*left*) poses challenges for civil engineers seeking to lay roads across its steep inclines, an example being the road Deralok as it snakes down into the valley.

Graves (*below*) of Mulla Mustafa Barzani (father to the current President of Kurdistan), and Idris Barzani (father to former Prime Minister Nechirvan Barzani), lie peacefully overlooking the now tranquil valley that stretches out below their home village of Barzan. A mausoleum stands not far from the graves – a site for pilgrims from across Kurdistan.

47

This cannon (*left and below*), standing in the town of Rowanduz, is one of two remaining cannons (the other in Baghdad) created by a Kurdish master craftsman who trained in weaponry in Russia. Inscribed to King Mohammad Bik and dated 1203 Hijri (1825), this would have been part of the defence against Ottoman forces seeking to conquer the Rowanduz Kingdom.

The attackers would not have had an easy task – like so many Kurdish villages, the vertiginous drops (*opposite*) place strict limits on the approaches that can be used. This drop of 1km to the valley floor below is known locally as 'Lover's Leap'.

and is widely believed to have been murdered. The Ottomans now seized total control, bringing to an end the Soran Emirate.

The first decades of the twentieth century saw a swift succession of foreign control of the town. In 1917, during the First World War, the town was destroyed by the Russians. In 1922 the town was occupied by the Turks, until they were driven out at the end of the year. On 22 April 1923, the British army took occupation of the town. The British decided to stay in place to await the arrival of a special commission to fix the border between Turkey and Iraq, believing that if they left the Turkish troops would return.

The occupants of Rowanduz have been the subject of a fair amount of travellers' interest. Archibald Milne Hamilton, architect of the famous 'Hamilton Road', commented on the amount of blood feuds that seemed to abound in the region: 'Rowanduz has always been a place of grim deeds and bloody retributions. Its greater and its lesser rulers alike have nearly all met with violent deaths and even today this reputation is being well earned.' The people of the town were shortly afterwards to become the subject of a full anthropological study as the

British army officer, Edmund Leach, visited Rowanduz in 1938, to study the Rowanduz Kurds as part of his thesis. His field trip had finally to be aborted for reasons beyond his control, but he nevertheless published his monograph 'Social and Economic Organization of the Rowanduz Kurds' two years later, an invaluable record of social life at that time.

In recent years, the town has undergone a fair amount of rebuilding, with the bazaar relocated to make way for a major new road. The town has grown, prospering like most of the Kurdistan Region, from the peace and an improved economic environment. The population today is estimated at something like 140,000.

Situated slightly further up the mountain from Rowanduz is the Pank tourist resort, a major new tourist infrastructure development for the region. Opened in 2007, it is the first such resort in Iraq and includes a Ferris wheel and other rides, along with a railed toboggan. With a large number of individual self-catering family villas, restaurants, swimming pools, saunas, tennis courts, helipads and mini golf courses, it is quite unlike any other resort in Iraq today.

The Pank resort *(above, left and right)* sits high on the mountain tops and represents a significant private investment in Kurdistan's growing tourism sector. The self-catering holiday chalets here provide a scenic getaway, with Ferris wheel, roller coaster and a restaurant with terrace for dining out at night. Views from this craggy peak look down to the Bekhar valley, a vertiginous 1km drop below.

Another tourist favourite – of long-standing – is the waterfall at Gali Ali Beg in the valley beneath Amediye *(left)* with a restaurant and cafe that straddles the water to cool weary feet. An illustration of this scene features on one of the Iraqi banknotes.

Further along the valley *(right)* sheep graze unattended by a donkey, a timeless reminder of a rural lifestyle that goes back, largely unchanged, to biblical times.

The village of Aboucha nestles between two small mountains *(next spread)*, the first village on the Speek plain as the traveller descends from the commanding position of the Iraqi military garrison.

The caravanserai in downtown Suleimaniah *(above)* is one of the oldest structures in the town. Although it has fallen into disrepair in recent years and its upper floors are now only used for storage, the arches of its ground floor serve to house the lively trade of fruitsellers pitching their wares to shoppers as they enter the bazaar.

The park in the centre of Suleimaniah *(above right)* is a popular picnic spot and rendezvous, with its central thoroughfare proudly carrying the busts of great Kurdish poets and writers through the ages.

The rural economy of Kurdistan centres itself naturally on market towns, scattered at intervals through the mountains. One such is the town of Qaladze, also known as Qala Diza, lying to the north of Suleimaniah. The name literally means 'Castle of Two Rivers' and refers to a small hill between two rivers that lies to the south-west of the town. With some 70,000 inhabitants, Qaladze is a regional hub for the surrounding mountain villages. Another such town is Ranye, capital of the local district, and located some 130km to the north-east of Suleimaniah, close to Lake Dukan. The inhabitants are known for the active roles they played in the Kurdish nationalist movements, not only at the time of the British occupation, but also in the 1991 insurgency against Saddam Hussein's regime. This fierce spirit of independence led to the town earning the popular name 'the Gate of Uprising'. Ranye is popular with tourists who come for the attractive water springs – one of which runs through the main bazaar – and for the picturesque local villages in the Dola Raqa valley. Ranye also boasts the remains of a castle, and a number of

archaeological sites nearby. The fertile soil of the region yields good crops, principally sunflowers, tobacco, rice, wheat and barley.

Down from Ranye lies the largest lake in Kurdistan, Lake Dukan, also known as 'Dokan'. This massive reservoir gathers waters from the Little Zab River, and directs it through to the powerful hydroelectric turbines of the Dukan dam, generating more than 400 MW of power feeding directly into the national grid.

Not far from here is Koi Sanjaq, much in the news as one of the epicentres of KDP/PUK skirmishes in the 1990s. Today, the town is prosperous and peaceful, a centre for the local agriculture.

Further east, and some 12 kilometres from the Iranian border lies the town of Halabja, tragically made internationally famous for the headline-grabbing poison-gas attacks under Saddam Hussein's regime, described in this volume towards the end of the history chapter. Halabja is a relatively modern town, built in around 1850 under Ottoman rule. One of the oldest buildings in the modern town is its central post office, opened in 1924, with the

Tea plays a vital role in social life, be it the street vendors offering beverages to passers-by near the park. (note the statue of one of the four generals of the Mahabad Republic behind) *(above left)*, or the gathered townspeople sipping in one of the famous literary cafes off Mawlawi street *(above)*.

first school opened nearby the following year. The Qaysari Pasha and Hamid Bag bazaars were built in 1932. Electricity did not reach the city until 1940. The city has recovered well from the agonies of the gas attacks in 1988, although there was some unrest in 2006 as a result of frustration with the administration for lack of progress on infrastructure projects. The city is scheduled to have its own airport which will doubtless encourage further economic development.

This whole eastern region has, through the centuries, been subject to the generally unwelcome attentions of the larger powers to the east and west. The notorious Nader Shah (1698 – 1747), ruler of Persia and founder of the Afsharid dynasty, had already directed huge energies to extend his dominions into the region, pressing the Kurdish principalities for their support. He was assassinated at the height of his powers before he could every quite realise his ambition of equalling Genghis Khan's breadth of conquest, but, in time, pressures came from the opposite direction, with the forces of the Ottoman ruler Mahmud II (1785

– 1839) becoming the scourge of the Kurdish principalities of the region. It was Ibrhaim Pasha, Prince of Baban, who finally established the town of Suleimaniah, naming it after his father Sulaiman Pasha. The town was carefully sited in a bowl between the various mountain ranges: Azmar, Goizha and Qaiwan, with Baranan Mountain to the south and the Tasluja hills to the west. Bazaars (Qasariyahs), palaces and public baths were constructed, and the town grew rapidly, establishing itself as the region's capital. The town's name is today variously spelled, but often known locally as "Slemany".

In time, Britain established itself as the dominant force in the region, occupying Iraq, but by the end of the First World War Kurdish nationalist sentiment in Suleimaniah sparked the first rebellion, led by Sheikh Mahmoud Barzanji in 1919. By 1921 the independent Kingdom of Kurdistan had been declared, with Suleimaniah as its capital. Shaikh Mahmoud Barzanji, with a degree of British support, declared himself King. British hopes that he might serve as some puppet ruler, a fig leaf for

Suleimaniah has a vivacious cultural life demonstrated in the activities of townspeople from all walks of life *(opposite)*. The students on the campus of the university are set to play a role in the Kurdish intelligentsia of the future. Debate and freedom of expression are now taken as a given. Passers-by in the street can browse from a range of local publications or attend a range of art galleries such as the one shown in the centre. The artisans supporting artists in the studio *(bottom right)* will have known less easy times; the studio itself was the notorious detention headquarters of the former regime into which a great many dissidents were taken, never to be seen again.

One of the highlights of Suleimaniah is the sweet bazaar *(right)*, centred around the famous Tawfik Halwachi store. Although many of the sweets are no longer made on the premises (the art of creating these culinary titbits has moved to workshops in the suburbs), the shops still tantalise shoppers, young and old alike, with their bright displays – lurid designs which distinguish them from rival sweetmakers of the Middle East.

Beyond Suleimaniah the mountains roll over into Iran, a rugged landscape shown here *(overleaf)* from Tawila.

the independence movement, quelling the insurgency, were soon to be dashed as Sheikh Mahmoud Barzanji insisted on ruling independently. He was promptly exiled by the British to India, only to return again in 1923 and lead a further rebellion based in Suleimaniah. He was unsuccessful, and the area became subsumed into the newly created state of Iraq, although Suleimaniah was to enjoy a period of greater autonomy that cities such as Erbil or Mosul further west.

Today, the town is capital of the governorate and is Iraqi Kurdistan's second city, with a population of around 800,000. Where Erbil stands as the seat of KRG government, with the parliament and new communities of international business residents, Suleimaniah has established itself as the centre for traditional culture and the arts.

Development of Sorani as a modern literary language started in this city in the early nineteenth century, when many Kurdish poets and men of letters like Nalî, Piramerd, Abdulla Goran, Muhamad Salih Dilan, Ahmad Hardi, Ibrahim Ahmad, Sherko Bekas and Bachtyar Ali lived or were published here.

Suleimaniah's main museum is located on Salim avenue, the city's central cafe-lined thoroughfare and it contains many valuable Mesopotamian artefacts. The cafe scene outside is lively, with debate very much alive and a community of artists who contribute to the various new galleries that have sprung up around the town. Galleries such as Zamoa and Aram showcase the best modern Kurdish art, with the Hall of Art and the Hall of Culture also hosting displays and international concerts. The recently formed National Youth Orchestra of Iraq held its initial concert in Suleimaniah, with over thirty Iraqi musicians forming the orchestra.

Suleimaniah embraces world music today, and there is a lively modern music scene with artists performing both traditional Kurdish dance songs and also modern rap and hip-hop variations.

Hand in hand with the inhabitants' enthusiasm for art and culture comes a reputation for liberal self-expression. The only two independent newspapers *Hawlati* and *Awena* are published in Suleimaniah.

The city is home to three universities. The original University of Sulaimani, opened in 1968 and teaching Engineering, Agriculture, Arts, Science, and Medicine, was relocated to Erbil in the late 1980s, renamed there as University of Salahaddin. To replace it, a new University of Suleimaniah was set up in 1991, much along the same lines as the former university. The second is the new American University of Sulaimani, with the sole medium of instruction being English. The third is the University of Human Development, opened in Qaradagh in 2008.

Economically, the city is flourishing. As ever it benefits from the local agricultural trade the area around Suleimaniah, and indeed across the governorate is known for its fertile soil, with plains such as Sharazoor and Bitwen yielding plentiful supplies of wheat and other agricultural produce.

In recent years, this revenue has been augmented by income from the increasing number of businesses located in the city, and from wider trade across Kurdistan and with Iran. Suleimaniah International Airport opened in 2005 bringing passengers and cargo from various eastern and European destinations such as Vienna, Frankfurt, Stockholm, Munich and Düsseldorf as well as the obvious Middle Eastern cities of the region.

2 |

FAITH

The majority of Kurds are Sunni Muslims from the Shafii school of Islam. There are also small numbers of Shias and communities of Sufis, particularly of the Naqshbandi order.

But Kurdish society is characterised by a strong degree of religious diversity, and there are many other groups besides Muslims. The Yezidis practise a syncretic faith, combining elements of Christian, Muslim and ancient Near Eastern religious traditions. The Shabaks are another group with their own distinctive syncretic faith and there are also several different Christian sects.

The village of Akre, in the mountains to the north-west of Erbil, is situated in a natural amphitheatre with the high minaret of the mosque rising at its centre.

Above:

Kurdish society is diverse and tolerant and home to many different religious groups. This selection of carpets laid out at a stall against the walls of Erbil's ancient citadel illustrates this, with iconography and symbols from across the broad spectrum of Kurdistan's religious communities.

Opposite:

This small mosque in the foothills below Rowanduz is typical of the many that can be found nestling off the beaten track. They are testament to the importance of faith in day-to-day life, although government building regulations now seek to limit the quantity being erected to pre-empt wider village construction in their wake.

In contrast to the situation in several parts of the surrounding region, Iraqi Kurdistan celebrates its religious diversity while at the same time manifesting certain elements of secularism. That is particularly true in the traditionally liberal city of Suleimaniah, which even boats a casino, something that would be frowned on in more conservative Islamic societies. Although a majority of Kurdistan's population is Sunni Muslim, notably from the Shafi'i school, a wide range of religious faiths and practices is represented within the population and many people have moved into Kurdistan to take advantage of the relative freedom of worship and greater personal security there compared with other parts of Iraq and neighbouring countries. The regional government believes that religious diversity and mutual tolerance and respect are essential elements of a mature democratic system, and actively encourages them.

As Prime Minister Nechirvan Barzani told an interfaith religious leaders' conference in Erbil in February 2009, 'Divine religions carry the message of peace, coexistence and tolerance. In the history of our people there have never been any issues or conflicts between Muslims and other religions in the Kurdistan Region. On the contrary, all the believers from all the religions in the Kurdistan Region have lived together as brothers and respect each other's beliefs. We are pleased that a large community of Christians live in the Kurdistan Region and have been here since the beginning of Christianity – long before the emergence of Islam.' He added, 'Islam and other divine religions in general educate human beings and guide them so that they are faithful, honest and merciful to their own people. There is an important point that we should remember at all times: When we were suffering and facing difficulties, we were all together . . . The chemical weapons which were used against our people [by Saddam Hussein] did not discriminate among Muslims, Christians, Yezidis, or among Kurds, Assyrians, Chaldeans, Syriacs or Turkmen.'

During the Ba'athist regime of Saddam Hussein, when Kurdish villages were being destroyed and local mosques blown up, religious leaders were among those individuals who dared to stand up and protest. In fact, both Muslim and Christian leaders had already been active in the so-called 'September Revolution' of 1960 to 1975, playing a leading role within their communities. Their religious messages at the time not only focussed on humanitarian issues but also embodied the spirit of the Kurdish liberation struggle. It was during that period that the late Mustafa Barzani founded the Religious Scholars Union, which attempted to foster harmony among the different religious authorities so that they could speak with one voice on matters of both faith and national concerns.

The predominant faith in the Region for the past few centuries has nonetheless been Sunni Islam and many of the region's laws have their roots in the Islamic faith. While some Kurdish secularists worry about the possible incorporation of shariah into the regional constitution, as sought by some Islamic parties, a large number of people attend mosques regularly and Muslim religious leaders enjoy considerable influence within society. The regional government provides services to imams working at the mosques through the Ministry of Endowment and Religious Affairs, as well as aiding the construction and rehabilitation of places of worship. It actively encourages progressive Islamic education, which is designed to foster peaceful coexistence, a love of the homeland and mutual respect between people as part of the school curriculum, while discouraging the use of religious platforms to propagate dissension and unrest, or the sort of religious fundamentalism and sectarianism that has plagued some other parts of Iraq.

The Shafi'i school of Islamic thought, which has its largest concentration anywhere in the world among the Kurds of Kurdistan, is one of four principal schools of religious law (*fiqh*) within Sunni Islam. It derives its name from Imam Muhammad ibn Idris ash-Shafi'i, who was reportedly born in Gaza around 150AH (AD 760). His original contribution, at a time when pragmatists of the Medina school were hotly debating theology with traditionalists, was to devise a system of systematic reasoning, without relying on personal deduction. He maintained that the only authoritative Sunnah (habits or usual practices) were those handed down from the Prophet Muhammad himself and he decreed that any Sunnah which contradicted what was written in the Holy Qur'an were unacceptable. During his lifetime, he was considered a heretic by some of his theological rivals and he was imprisoned for a while, as well as being transported to Baghdad at one stage, in humiliation and disgrace. But later Imam ash-Shafi'i's book *Al-Risalah* was widely acknowledged to be the foundation for Islamic jurisprudence and Shafi'i teaching has broad appeal in much of the Islamic world. As well as winning acceptance as a religious authority, Imam ash-Shafi'i gained a high reputation as a poet, one of his best-known verses (rendered into English by Salma el-Helali) being:

We blame our time, though we are to blame.
No fault has time but only us –

We scold the time for all the shame.
Had it a tongue, it would scold us.

Traditional mosque architecture in Kurdistan reflects two main influences: Iranian and Ottoman, the latter drawing heavily on Byzantine traditions. Among the most celebrated of the older mosques in the Kurdistan Region is the Great Mosque of Hewler (Erbil), also known as the White Mosque or the Citadel Mosque, which was built in the eighth century by the princes of the Baban principality and renovated in the early years of the twentieth century by Abu Bakr Mulla Afandi, whose father had preached there. Mulla Afandi succeeded his father on the latter's death, and because of his great learning, became the sole source of religious decrees or fatwas in Erbil and the surrounding districts.

A remarkable polymath, Abu Bakr Mulla Afandi taught not only Islamic philosophy and history, but also Ethics, Science, Astronomy and Mathematics and issued over one hundred scientific licences to scholars across Mesopotamia, Persia and the wider Middle East.

Inside the colourfully decorated Great Mosque there is a shrine to Kak Ahmedi Sheikh, a renowned Islamic cleric from the Qadiri order (one of the oldest Sufi *tariqas*), as well as a shrine to the Kurdish nationalist leader Sheikh Mahmud Alhafeed.

Until well into the twentieth century, only the mullas and a small number of independent

Left:
The elegant minaret shown here is typical of the design used across Iraqi Kurdistan — a classical structure similar to the style in Turkey.

Right:
Al-Gawra Mosque in Suleimaniah sits above a busy square where merchants and tea-sellers abound.

scholars in Kurdistan were literate and so most education took place in the mosques and associated madrasas or religious schools, where religious instruction was available for boys from the age of seven (girls usually received only limited teaching at home, if at all). The texts used as the basis of religious instruction were in Arabic, but much of the classroom work was carried out in Kurdish. In the absence of government bureaucracy, mullas often filled judicial roles within the community, as well as registering births, deaths, marriages and so on.

Sufism continues to play an important part in the religious life of Kurdistan, especially among those who are more attracted to the mystical side of the Islamic faith. While all Muslims believe that during their life they are on a pathway to God and that they will ultimately come close to him in Paradise, if they live a worthy existence on this earth, Sufis argue that it is possible to draw closer to God in the here and now. In principle, all Sufis seek to please the Almighty by returning themselves to a primordial state (*fitra*), as described in the Holy Qur'an. When one is in that state, everything is undertaken with the single motivation of one's love of God. In order to attain this state, a devotee first needs to identify a suitable teacher, who should in principle be part of an unbroken succession of Masters of the Way stretching all the way back to the Prophet Muhammad. According to the Sufi tradition, the student learns not so much from book learning but by the transmission of the divine light and understanding from his teacher's heart into his own. Over a period of many years, a close relationship develops between pupil and master and the latter will prescribe practices which should help the student achieve his goal. Often that will involve aspects of self-imposed asceticism, including silence, solitude, sleeplessness and hunger. In Turkey and Sudan and several other parts of the world where Sufism is prevalent, some orders practise not only meditation but also group worship in the form of singing, instrumental music, dance and the use of trance – most famously among the so-called 'whirling dervishes' of the Mevlevi order.

In Kurdistan, the followers of some Sufi orders enter a state of ecstasy in which they perform extreme bodily feats such as swallowing swords, eating light bulbs, fire-eating and piercing metal skewers through their flesh, as their companions beat drums and chant the name of Allah. The religious shrines in Berzanchi, a village about 60 kilometres east of Suleimaniah, sometimes attract a crowd of thousands for such ritual festivals, in which the participants say they feel neither fear nor pain and that while they are inflicting these

extraordinary demands on their mortal flesh, their hearts will be with God. The idea is that the soul can transcend the body at the will of a well-trained mind. A local Sufi leader, Sheikh Qadir Kaka Hanna, comments more prosaically, 'When a Sufi cuts himself, with the help of God, his wounds will heal.'

A significant number of inhabitants of the Kurdish Region are affiliated to the Naqshbandi order of Sufism. This is partly thanks to the legacy of an energetic nineteenth century sheikh by the name of Mawlana Khalid, from Shahrazur (modern Suleimaniah), who proselytised widely and successfully across the region. Accordingly, Sufi 'lodges' can be found

throughout the area, in some places even more commonly than mosques.

Islam in its many forms has never enjoyed a monopoly of adherents in the Region. Judaism also has a long history in Kurdistan, though it is now virtually extinct because of emigration. The first Jews reportedly came into the Region briefly in the eighth century BC, when the Assyrians defeated the Kingdom of Israel. Seven hundred years later, King Monobazes and the rest of the royal house of Adiabene, which had its capital at Erbil, converted to Judaism and started to proselytise among the local population.

Subsequently, significant Jewish communities developed in the Region, some of them – notably the important business families of Mosul – enjoying considerable autonomy in the running of their affairs. For centuries, they lived under the protection of tribal chieftains or aghas, to whom they would sometimes offer tribute or gifts, or commissions on their commercial transactions. The Jewish community tended to marry within itself and was quite closed to the world outside. It produced not just successful merchants but also some distinguished religious authorities,

including the female Talmud scholar and poet, Asenath Barzani, who enjoyed a long life in Mosul in the seventeenth century, heading the yeshivah or religious school at Amediye and eventually becoming the most respected teacher of the Torah in all of Kurdistan. Unlike most Kurdish Jews, she knew Hebrew fluently; the common language of most Kurdish Jews was Aramaic, which is what Jesus probably spoke. The community observed Jewish law quite strictly and regularly attended synagogues, where the moral principles and rituals of the religion were passed on from one generation to the next orally, notably through sermons by rabbis who were the most important figures in their community.

Jews in Kurdistan were traditionally buried in graves with their feet pointing towards Jerusalem, probably in the hope that this would hasten their arrival there on the Day of Judgment. They kept alive their historic attachment to the biblical land of Israel and even gave biblical names to some Kurdish towns. Zakho they referred to as 'the Jerusalem of Kurdistan', for example. Some Kurdish Jews were active in the Zionist movement in the late nineteenth and early twentieth centuries and moved to Palestine when it was under the British Mandate. In 1951–52, following the first Israeli–Arab war, most of the remaining Kurdish Jews left to live in the new state of Israel, where they have tried to preserve their

distinctive culture. However, important Jewish shrines remain in Kurdistan, notably the supposed tombs of several biblical prophets, including Daniel at Kirkuk, Jonah at Nabi Yunis (ancient Nineveh) and Nahum at Alikush.

It has to be admitted that at least half a dozen places in the Middle East claim to house Daniel's tomb, but Kirkuk's case is one of the strongest, as the city was the prophet's home town. The tomb is located in the citadel, on the site of what was originally a Jewish temple before becoming a Christian church and finally a mosque. Kirkuk's reputation as a place that honoured the followers of all three 'religions of the Book' (as they are called by Muslims) was so

Opposite:
The principal colour of the Yezidi faith is white, said to represent purity. All spiritually devout people as well as religious dignitaries wear white.

Above:
Yezidi men are known for their long moustaches, which, according to the tenets of the faith, they are forbidden to cut. In the background is the Yezidi temple at Lalish, characterised by its distinctive conical roof.

great that many people chose to be buried there near to Daniel's tomb. Local historians believe the graveyard attached to the mosque at Kirkuk is the oldest cemetery in the area. The citadel suffered considerable depredation in recent decades.

Judaism was by no means the most ancient religious tradition in the area, however. The Yezedis could certainly claim that honour. Kurdistan houses the greatest concentration of Yezidis anywhere in the world, though it is hard to establish exact numbers as some adherents are secretive about their beliefs. Yezidis – or Ezidis, as they sometimes prefer to call themselves – espouse a faith that has its roots in Near Eastern prehistory, drawing on traditions

and practices that date from ancient Mesopotamian and Persian customs, Zoroastrianism, early Christianity and even mainstream Islam. The syncretic character of Yezidism is further complicated by the undoubted influence of Sufism. Within Yezidi terminology, there is plenty of Sufi imagery, but much of the community's mythology is distinctly pre-Islamic, what earlier Western scholars would once have referred to dismissively as 'pagan'. Though there is still academic debate about the exact nature and provenance of Yezidism, when one considers the medieval history of Kurdistan it would appear that members of the Adawiyya Sufi order living up in the Kurdish mountains came

under the influence of older religious concepts prevalent in the area. The founder of the Adawiyya Order, Adi ibn Musafir, actually settled in the valley of Lalish, about fifty kilometres north-east of Mosul, and, after he died in 1162, his tomb became a site of Yezidi pilgrimage, as it still is today. If possible, all Yezidis are supposed to make at least one pilgrimage to Lalish during their lifetime, rather as Muslims do to Mecca and Medina on the hajj.

In a nutshell, most Yezidis believe that God created the world, and that He is now in the care of seven Holy Beings (the figure seven has mystic significance in several religions and popular traditions), of whom the most important is Tawuse Melek, an angel usually colourfully depicted as a beautiful peacock with his tail feathers fully displayed. Tawuse Melek

also goes under another name, Shaytan, which in Arabic means 'devil', which is why many Muslims – who have often looked down on the Yezidis – sometimes refer to them as 'devil-worshippers'. Like Muslims, Yezidis pray five times a day, but instead of looking towards Mecca they pray facing the sun, which accounts for their other popular name, the 'sun-worshippers'. They are traditionally quite a closed community, marrying among themselves and in principle non-Yezidis are excluded from their ceremonies. As part of their concern for religious purity, they have strict dietary laws and they also maintain a sort of caste system within their community. Many Yezidis believe in reincarnation and it is written in their holy books that human beings are descendants of Adam, though not, intriguingly, of Eve.

Newroz is one of the most important festivals in Kurdistan's calendar. Here light is being carried down from the hillside into the Lalish temple (*above and opposite*). The light that burns during the New Year festival commemorates the arrival of light into the world. The festival is a joyous and celebratory occasion; it also features music, communal dancing and lavish banquets.

Somewhat related to the Yezidis is a small ethno-religious group called the Shabak, who live in several villages to the east of Mosul. They have their own language, called Shabaki, which is considered to be part of the Zaza-Gorani group, which is in turn related to Kurdish, but with borrowings from several other regional languages. Like the Yezidis – to whose shrines they often go on pilgrimage – the Shabaks follow a syncretic belief system, which embraces elements of Islam, Christianity and other religions.

Moreover, despite the relatively small total number of adherents, the faith is divided into three distinct groups or denominations. The Shabaks' sacred book, the *Buyruk*, is written in colloquial Iraqi Turkmen. Sufi influence led the Shabaks to adopt a more mystical and intuitive interpretation of divine lore than that of their Muslim neighbours and several of their practices are quite distinctive. These include making confessions, both in private and in public, and also permitting the drinking of alcohol. Spiritual guides or *pir*, who are well versed in the sect's beliefs and rituals, act as intermediaries between the deity and adherents of the religion; above these *pir* is the *baba* or supreme leader. The Shabaks were particularly targeted during the notorious Anfal campaign of 1988 and transported along with various other minority groups to resettlement camps in other parts of Iraq, where they came under intense pressure to Arabise. But many later returned to their place of origin where they have tried to rebuild their communities along traditional lines and to reaffirm their beliefs.

With regard to Christianity, Kurdistan is home to a number of different Churches, including Syrian Catholic, Syrian Orthodox, the Assyrian Church of the East, Armenian and Catholic Chaldean. According to Coptic sources, it was St Andrew who first led Christian missionary efforts among the Kurds in the sixth century, finding converts among the sun-worshippers. Over the centuries there was also quite a lot of two-way conversion between Christianity and Islam, despite the latter's teaching on apostasy.

Many of the early Kurdish Christian converts were Nestorian and worshipped separately from the Assyrians and Armenians, but, in more recent times, missionary activity has come largely from European and American Protestant denominations, including the Lutherans. Christian relief agencies were involved in charitable work among Iraqi Kurds following the First Gulf War of 1991 and the subsequent reprisals by the central government, and, after 2000, the KRG allowed various evangelical Christian groups to operate in the territory. Since then there has been a Kurdish-speaking evangelical church operating in the region, called the Kurdzman Church of Christ, which

Mar Matti Monastery (Saint Matthew's Monastery) (*left, below and opposite*) stands atop Mount Maqloub in the north-west of Kurdistan some 20 kilometres from Mosul. It was founded in AD 363 by a Syriac Christian called Matti (Syriac for Matthew) who was fleeing persecution from Diyarbakır. Matti joined a mostly Nestorian population that had a small Syrian community already located on Mount Maqloub and led the community into a true monastic ethos. It is today recognized as one of the oldest Christian monasteries in existence and is noted for its considerable collection of Syriac Christian manuscripts.

was originally found only in Erbil, but now has branches in Suleimaniah, Kirkuk and Dohuk as well.

Christian activity is not limited to churches or evangelism. For example, Servant Group International, a US-based non-profit Christian organisation, runs three schools in the Region, each called Classical School of the Medes, which has as its motto 'Rebuilding Iraq, one child at a time'. Over 95% of the pupils in these schools are Kurdish Muslims, who study alongside followers of Orthodox and evangelical Christianity as well as other religious traditions. These schools employ an English-language curriculum which has as its core educational philosophy the belief that the purpose of education is to preserve, refine and transmit values from one generation to the next. The schools incorporate a Christian world-view, which the Classical School of the Medes defines as a foundation for constitutional democracy, religious freedom and tolerance. It aims to present all this in a culturally sensitive and appropriate manner, through the teaching of values such as truth, beauty and goodness, using a variety of sources, including the Bible. As a further sign of religious tolerance in the Region, The Bible Society has been granted an official permit to work in Kurdistan.

Since the Iraq War of 2003, many Christians in other parts of Iraq have been the targets of violent attacks from Islamic extremists, but in the Kurdistan Region the government has made strenuous efforts to avoid any such sectarian conflict. In 2009, three ministers in the government were of Assyrian or Chaldean origin and in elections to the Kurdish National Assembly five seats were allocated to Christians. According to official sources, since 1991 Assyrians and Chaldeans have, moreover, been able to publish newspapers and broadcast in their own languages as well as establishing their own political parties. There are more than thirty Assyrian language schools in the KRG area and about twenty Assyrian churches have been restored or repaired.

The Assyrians are one of Iraq's most ancient religious groups, following the Eastern Orthodox Christian tradition. However, large numbers of Assyrians have been forced to flee their traditional home in Arab Iraq. Five Assyrian churches were bombed in Baghdad in July 2009 and there have been killings in Mosul, just outside the KRG's area of control. Some of the Assyrian refugees – including priests – have moved abroad, but many thousands have found sanctuary in Kurdistan. At Ainkawa, a district of Erbil, there are several

large Assyrian churches and a burgeoning Assyrian community, including restaurants and shops selling alcohol, a trade they had previously dominated in Baghdad. A giant poster of Pope Benedict XVI greeting Kurdish President Masoud Barzani looks down over the main road intersection leading into Ainkawa, symbolising the government's outreach to the region's Christian minorities. The authorities' stated aim in Kurdistan – which has certain spiritual overtones, despite its declared secularism – is to secure the safety of the Region and a better future for its people, based on shared values and principles, so that a democratic, pluralist, secular and federal system

operating in the basis of cooperation and consensus can be firmly established within the wider framework of Iraq. Religious tolerance is specifically championed as a symbol of civilised and successful societies. As Prime Minister Nechirvan Barzani comments, 'We have never allowed religious and sectarian differences to make us weak. In fact, the diversity among us became a source of strength and power in the Kurdistan Region.'

3

SOCIETY & CULTURE

s an ancient people, the Kurds have a rich and deep cultural identity which for centuries has been revered and nurtured with pride. Today, despite the fact that its people are spread between several different states, the traditional bonds in Kurdish society are strong and Kurdish culture is as dynamic a force as ever. Kurdish music and other art forms are enjoyed and appreciated not just among the Kurds themselves, but also by the peoples of the wider region to which they belong.

The elderly Kurd here is wearing the traditional Kurdish dress of the north-west as he looks down from the mountain top west of Dohuk.

Despite their varied and sometimes disputed origins, the Kurdish people have developed over the centuries distinctive, common social characteristics and forms of cultural expression. Even though the traditional Kurdish lands have been divided among four different foreign states for the last eight decades, and even though national governments have at one time or another tried to undermine or deny Kurdish identity, strong elements of that social and cultural identity have survived. As befits a people of nomadic background, the Kurds have often migrated between the four countries of Iraq, Iran, Turkey and Syria, sometimes voluntarily, sometimes out of necessity. Others have found sanctuary or economic opportunity much further afield: in Britain, Germany, Sweden, North America and even Australia. The Kurdish diaspora generally keeps in close touch with developments back home, through personal contacts and a variety of satellite TV channels and other media, though they have inevitably been influenced by the alien societies in which they have settled, some of which have very different values and social norms from their own. Within Kurdistan itself, forced resettlement, urbanisation and modernisation have all contributed to pressures for change.

The negative effects of that change often manifest themselves as a sense of loss. A bittersweet nostalgia for a vanished past pervades not just the literature and performing arts of the Kurds but also some of the dynamics within Kurdish families and communities. Though cultural tensions may be superficially invisible in a thrusting city like Suleimaniah, one does not have to probe far to uncover different expectations between generations as well as between those who have willingly embraced a certain degree of Westernisation and those who struggle to retain or to disinter customs and beliefs from the past.

The sense of tribe and of family remains strong and the conservative values of a patriarchal society in which respect for older people and traditional gender roles is emphasised have been maintained. These include a deep sense of honour, both individually and collectively. This is particularly true when it relates to the comportment of unmarried girls within the family and in the outside world. Modesty in dress and behaviour is expected in women, just as bravery and loyalty are qualities praised in men. Any divergence from expected norms traditionally brings terrible vengeance upon the 'guilty' party, usually from within the family itself, as it asserts its collective authority and wipes out perceived shame by whatever means it deemed necessary. These tribal values and principles predate the arrival of Islam, though among the Muslim majority of southern (i.e. Iraqi) Kurds, the religion has reinforced earlier practices, particularly in communities or families in which there has been a recent revival of Islamic piety.

Even among more secular or less pious Kurds, the rigidity of gender distinctions and the manifestation of manly and womanly virtues endure. A man should be ready to fight when it is necessary to protect the homeland or the clan; the woman should be a competent mother and home manager. Daughters, in particular, should obey their parents. Though love marriages are less rare than they were a generation ago, the expectation is that a girl should marry someone chosen or at least approved of by her parents. She should preferably marry young and have many children; fertility is a cause for joy and is noticeably higher among Kurds than the norm of any of the majority ethnicities of the four major states in which they live. As the Kurdish musician Siamand Minehzadeh Morowatdost told the Australian journalist Gina Lennox in an interview 'girls must be quiet and listen to older women. They must not show their intelligence or have an open mind and they must not be honest about their feelings.' This is as true of other Kurdish regions as it is in his native east (i.e. Iranian) Kurdistan. Within the KRG, there has been a new emphasis on female education and emancipation, but old assumptions and practices die hard, even within the diaspora in Europe.

In the villages that were central to Kurdish lifestyles until so many thousands were destroyed in both Iraq and Turkey, a high degree of gender segregation was enforced within the household and the community. Although the youngest girls could accompany their parents on the visits to family and friends that formed such an important part of Kurdish life, after puberty (or even some time before) their movements were more restricted, unlike those of the boys. It was thus quite difficult for young men and girls to meet, except through family introductions, with the interesting exceptions of the dances which played an important role within community life, especially at times of celebration, such as Newroz, the Kurdish New Year or spring awakening. It is still usual on such occasions for Kurds to dance in circles or lines; a man will lead the line, waving a kerchief or other piece of material from his hand, as the other dancers, boys and girls mixed, follow. There will often be a singer or at least some musicians, playing traditional instruments such as a *simsal* or *kemenje* or *tapel*. As this is a communal activity, it is all perfectly respectable, but it does allow the young to see and chastely to touch each other. During such ceremonies, it is more common than in everyday life to see Kurds wearing traditional clothes: colourful, often sequined, long-sleeved dresses for young women, and usually more subdued hues for older women, who may nonetheless wear considerably more gold jewellery, which reflects their marital status and personal wealth. Women from more affluent families may also wear a belt made from loops of gold. The men traditionally wear baggy pants and various types of vest jackets, wide belts and sometimes checkered scarves like the Arab kaffiyeh, or the military garb of the Peshmaerga. However, Western dress is more common for men in

Opposite:
Kurds across the generations. For people from all backgrounds, across all ages, and in all parts of society, their Kurdish identity is a major feature of their lives.

should remain standing virtually motionless while they drink their water and make their assessment. If that has been favourable, they will return for a second visit, bringing the suitor with them. This means that at least the two people most concerned in the arrangements get a brief chance to get to know each other a little. In principle, the girl can reject the suitor, though this might result in strong criticism and pressure from her family if they approve of the man. If, on the contrary, she is enthusiastic about the prospective mate she must not show it, as to do so would be unseemly. If the man (who may be young but could be considerably older) is pleased, he indicates this to his companions who make a formal request to the girl's family. If this is accepted, wedding preparations move forward quickly. The groom gives his prospective bride a ring which she wears on her right hand, signalling that she is engaged to be married. Once the couple are wedded, the ring is transferred to the left hand, signalling that the couple are married and that the groom now has the right to visit his wife's family, while the other guests celebrate by

singing and dancing. The groom's family will offer gifts to their new in-laws and the festivities end with a shawl or *shara buke* being placed over the bride's head.

Given the patriarchal nature of traditional Kurdish society, not only do fathers and brothers have a degree of authority or control over a young woman, but her new husband also acquires rights which are generally recognised within the community. If things go badly in the marriage, the husband and his family will often declare that it is the wife's fault, whereas if things go well, then relatives and neighbours may comment that the man has trained her well. Of course, in the cities and among more modern families there is often a greater degree of equilibrium within the partnership and women have developed more assertiveness, especially in families or communities which have been influenced by Marxist or other socialist thought, or have studied or lived abroad, either in the former Soviet bloc or in the West.

There are some examples in Kurdish history of women who have attained positions of power

everyday life these days, especially at the workplace. At different times and in various parts of greater Kurdistan, men have actually been forbidden to wear Kurdish clothes in public.

Marriage is a central preoccupation of most Kurds' lives and traditional practices have dictated formalised procedures affecting every stage of the process from the marriage proposal through a short period of acknowledged engagement to the wedding ceremony itself. When a family identifies a suitable possible bride for one of its male members, it will send a small delegation of its usually older members to visit the girl's home. They make clear the purpose of their visit and if the girl's parents show at least some willingness to consider the proposition, the visitors then ask for some water, which is habitually served by the girl herself. This way, the potential groom's relatives get a chance to make a judgment about her appearance and character. In principle, she

Major social events such as weddings are important community occasions when local society gathers and reaffirms its bonds and solidarity. The wedding here (***opposite top***) is conducted in the open air by the river, as is the music festival (***opposite below***) and the marriage dance (***above***). Kurdish dance is traditionally done in a group, with hands held to form a circle. Singing and dance are a central feature of all birthdays, marriages and other celebrations.

in their own right, notably in the principalities that existed prior to the tightening of Ottoman control over the Kurds' affairs. In Iraq, the first publication specifically for Kurdish women, '*Dengi Afiret*', was launched and women successfully lobbied for changes in the law which meant that marriage came under civil legislation and so-called honour killings were officially outlawed. Honour killings involve the murder of a girl or woman who is considered to have shamed her family – for example, by engaging in a relationship (even unconsummated) with a man who has not been chosen for her. The father and/or brothers traditionally would carry out the killing, sometimes but not always with the mother's approval. Though the practice is illegal and condemned by the authorities, it is still occasionally reported to happen within very conservative families. Similarly, female circumcision is disapproved of by the

authorities, but is surprisingly common in Iraqi Kurdistan. Following the formation of the Kurdistan Regional Government, women gained new freedoms to form their own organisations and several have achieved positions of political authority within the region and beyond.

Newroz is the paramount Kurdish celebration, marked on or around 21 March, the spring equinox. It provides the pretext for parties that are as popular among the Kurdish diaspora in Europe and elsewhere as they are in the Kurdish territories. In the predominantly Kurdish areas of south-eastern Turkey, bordering the KRG region of Iraq, the Kurdish nationalist colours of green, yellow and red are worn and flags defiantly waved. Newroz songs and music celebrate the end of winter's cold, snow and driving rain or sleet and welcome the rebirth of green pastures and the rich tapestry of flowers which spreads out across the hillsides

Zoroastrianism), and in various parts, of Kurdistan young men will jump over fires as a demonstration of both their courage and the Kurds claim to freedom. Bonfires light up the night sky. The 1930s Kurdish poet Taufik Abdullah embellished the story of Kawa as part of his campaign to launch a Kurdish cultural revival. But one can find literary references to Newroz and its associated myths dating back much earlier. For example, the early seventeenth century poet Melaye Ciziri wrote:

Without the light and the fire of love
Without the Designer and the power
of the Creator
We are not able to reach union.

Festivities are marked not only with dancing and singing and dressing up in one's finest clothes, but also with special foods. If the spring weather is already mild, families may go into the hills with a picnic in which the favourite dish of yaprak or dolma often features. Vine leaves will be stuffed with rice that has been mixed with onion, garlic, herbs and spices, butter, maybe chilli and tomato paste, some vegetables such as capsicum and sometimes chopped, uncooked meat. A variant employs vegetables such as aubergines, courgettes, tomatoes or even potatoes and onions stuffed with the same kind of mixture and all cooked together in one pot.

These days, rice is often the staple food of Kurdish families, replacing the more traditional bulgur wheat, but to this rice is often added lamb and vegetables cooked slowly in a tomato-based sauce. Cucumber and salads are eaten in large quantities. Kurdish cuisine varies considerably from region to region, as well as according to season, but there are some famous, distinctive recipes, such as 'Kurdish chicken' – a gull pan-seared and then glazed with a paste made from dates.

The soil of the mountain regions has bounteous natural fertility – markets display produce (**opposite**) which will have been harvested locally. In rural districts grapes are laid on flat roofs to dry and turn in time into raisins (*above*).

and meadows. This natural period of change is seen as an opportune moment to divest oneself of the troubles and cares of the past (rather as in some European cultures, families would sweep out the old year from their house on New Year's Eve). Old disputes are meant to be put aside, grievances forgiven and relationships given a fresh impetus. Probably Persian in origin, the legends and customs associated with Newroz have been built on by Kurds and in some important ways transformed. One background

story relates to the monstrous, cannibalistic Zuhak (in some versions a giant, in others an Assyrian King who had snakes growing out of his shoulders), who not only chased the children who would become Kurds up into the mountains but also prevented spring from arriving. According to many versions of this story, Zuhak was killed by a heroic figure called Kawa, who then set fire to the hillside in celebration. Fire plays an important part in Newroz symbolism (underlining its links to

between layers of grass and leaves on wooden platforms built into trees. Tomatoes, peppers, aubergines, okra and other commodities could be sun-dried in autumn to prolong their usability.

On normal days, a Kurdish family will still start the day with a breakfast of flat bread, honey and yoghurt, washed down with black tea. The women of the household have the responsibility for preparing the food, though the men often do the shopping for those ingredients that are not produced by the family itself. Because most of the foodstuffs are locally sourced and fresh, and fruit and vegetables constitute such a significant part of the Kurds' diet, the traditional Kurdish lifestyle was considered by outsiders as being particularly healthy, especially taking into account the amount of exercise taken by the men in particular in the course of their daily activities and the purity of the mountain air and water. However, many Kurds reacted badly to the change of diet, climate and living conditions when they were resettled in other parts of Iraq or Turkey. To these physical adversities was added in many cases the trauma of dispossession, family deaths and even the adjustments necessary for living in an urban environment, sometimes provoking psychological as well as physical symptoms. That situation was made far worse in cases where Kurdish cultural expression was denied or restricted.

With regard to cultural expression, poetry is widely regarded as the highest form of literature among Kurds, as it is in Persian culture. This is not only because of the intensity of meaning and the beauty of language found in good poems but also because of poetry's central position in a cultural tradition that was essentially oral until recent times. Just as older people within their communities would pass on their traditions and survival skills to new generations by word of mouth, so poets would recite their work to attentive listeners, keeping the culture alive. Ordinary people could learn and quote favourite stanzas as well, so that these became part of the language of common

The mountains themselves for millennia offered a source of food to the Kurdish tribes, especially in spring when many types of mushrooms emerge as well as edible grasses and herbs. Later in the year there are wild berries and other fruits. Because of the seasonal nature of the climate, until recently food storage was of vital importance in Kurdish villages, and families would have enough provisions to last through the long winter. Potatoes and root vegetables such as turnips, radishes and beetroot could be buried under the earth floor of a dwelling, to be dug up as required, but more perishable foods required more delicate treatment. According to the chef and cookery writer Mosa Dashtani, fruit would be stored

The traditional way of life remains unchanged today in much of Kurdistan, especially the remoter rural villages. Bread is still baked in traditional clay ovens (*opposite top*) and is a fine accompaniment to a simple broth made from lentils and oats (*right*) served in pots hand cast by local artisans (*opposite left*). As across the entire region, a kettle of hot water is never far away and the traditional repast is washed down with sweet tea (*below right*).

discourse, along with proverbs and Qur'anic sayings (at least among Muslims). As in various other cultures, the poetry was and remains linked to songs, many of which would be transmitted through the Kurdish Region by travelling performers. Later, they were propagated by radio and more recently by television. Many of the songs are about love, both human longing for a beloved and spiritual longing for the divine, or indeed heartfelt passion for the homeland of the Kurds, with its mountain scenery, spring flowers, the snows of winter and other physical attributes that took on an almost sacred value in the popular consciousness. Just as the songs varied from place to place, so too did the musical instruments which accompanied them. These might range from a simple flute cut from sugar cane to intricate wind or string instruments that were professionally made to a high standard. According to Siamand Minehzadeh Morowatdost, flutes were played by young shepherds who looked after the sheep and the goats up in the mountain pastures. The solitude of this occupation was thought to encourage reflection on the meaning of life as well as providing inspiration for music.

In the twentieth century, a number of singers and musicians – some of whom were illiterate – made their own compositions, combining ancient folklore and themes with more modern concerns and nationalistic aspirations, or else they reprised long-forgotten poems. Of the Iraqi Kurds, singers such as Rasul Gardi, Ali Merdan and Tahir Tawfiq became famous among their compatriots. In the last century, an Iranian Kurd, Hasan Zirek, travelled widely in Iraq, performing. When the central government was engaging in rapprochement with the Kurds, he was often heard on the radio from Baghdad, but at other times he was imprisoned and maltreated. Some of his colleagues fared worse, as the Ba'athists turned the screw on cultural expression that was deemed subversive. The musician Erdewan Zaxoli, for example, was executed. Eventually Hasan Zirek returned to the comparative safety of Iran. Political dissidence (as perceived by the Iraqi Arab authorities) was not the only stigma some Kurdish performers had to bear. For many people within the wider Kurdish community itself, musicians were dangerously unfettered by the conventions and norms of society. Just as the Peshmergas were admired for confronting death fearlessly in their armed struggle, so in counterpoint the musicians were often viewed askance for doing what they wanted or believed in, without caring what other people thought.

Formerly, traditional performers were classified into three types which have been translated into English terminology as minstrels, storytellers and bards. During those historical periods in which there were Kurdish princely courts, musicians would be called on to provide entertainment in the evenings and the most popular songs were often those that were based on epic poems or legends. The different genres of songs were similarly defined, including heroic ballads, wistful laments over unrequited love, religious music and wedding songs, for example.

One type was specifically related to the melancholy of autumn; like the spring of Newroz, the autumn's heralding of shorter, colder days leading to bitter winter was a transitional period for a collective response in a culture so closely tied to the land, as well as being in an area of climatic extremes. In summer, the heat would be so oppressive that people would sleep on the roofs of their houses, while in winter the cold would be so intense that movement outside was restricted and the prime concern for people was keeping warm and having enough fuel to cook hot food. Life could be very hard under such conditions, which is one reason why some Kurds migrated voluntarily to urban centres and aspired to a more affluent lifestyle, in which air-conditioning and more efficient heating systems were available.

It is always unwise to generalise too much, especially when it comes to a people as varied in their origins and living conditions as the Kurds are today. That diversity is even reflected in the language that they speak. Iraqi efforts to Arabise parts of southern Kurdistan, like Turkish efforts to 'Turkify' Kurdish areas, have often meant that people have lost the ability to communicate properly in Kurdish, though that has been less true of Iraqi Kurdistan than it is in Turkey. But in linguistic terms, the very word 'Kurdish' is problematic, as there is no single variant that is common to all Kurds. Instead, a number of Kurdish and related dialects tend to be classified into two main groups, often referred to as Badini and Sorani. To complicate matters further, the former has tended to be written in Arabic script, while the latter uses the Latin alphabet or, in Armenia, Georgia and Russia where there are Kurdish minorities, Cyrillic script. There was a pre-Islamic Kurdish

The arts, indigenous and foreign, are alive and thriving in Kurdistan: Aziz Waisi is among the most beloved and renowned singers in the Kurdistan Region (***below***) while men and women perform at the annual festival of ballet at Erbil (***above***). The pop star Dashni Murad (***opposite***) brings a brand of music that blends American pop in the style of Shakira with traditional folk themes.

alphabet which is now only decipherable to specialist scholars. But intellectuals such as the writer and editor Abdulwahab Talabani hope that some sort of unified literary standard might be agreed which would help disseminate the people's rich cultural legacy. In the meantime, Kurdish radio and television often employ a variety of regional dialects unless broadcasting a very restricted area.

Abdulwahab Talabani, who has translated many Kurdish poems and short stories into Arabic, as well as publishing original work of his own, has highlighted the importance of morality tales as a component of the oral tradition which helps preserve and transmit values and norms that can assist cultural and community cohesion. Many of these tales, rather like the fables of Aesop, feature anthropomorphic animals who act out the tragedies and comedies of human life, the lessons learned implying the limitless nature of contrasting experiences such as suffering and love. Sometimes, the two emotions are combined into one, rather as in Shakespeare's Romeo and Juliet. These Kurdish folkloric tales reverberate with the physical and emotional sensations of a nomadic existence divided between summer pastures and winter settlements, as well as the values of male friendship and the troubling but delicious challenges of a special relationship across the deep gender divide.

Such cultural expression is helping Kurdish society rediscover its roots after many decades of disturbance and change. But it would be wrong to think that all political, economic and social change has been negative for Kurdish society. Far from it. Greater wealth and access to education – for women as well as men – have opened up new opportunities for individuals and families as well as providing them with more security. From the sociologist's point of view, a less visible but nonetheless significant aspect of the transformation that has been happening in Kurdistan is the way that people's prime loyalties are no longer exclusively towards family, clan or community, but increasingly also towards civic entities of various kinds. The twentieth century growth of consciousness of a

Kurdish ethno-nationalist identity – paradoxically partly in response to attempts by others to deny it – made a profound change to the general context of 'Kurdishness'. The party political system that emerged in the 1970s – dominated by the KDP and the PUK – led to a reappraisal of loyalties, no longer along clan lines, though these remained important. And the horrors of the Anfal Campaign waged against Kurds by the Ba'athist government in the 1980s assisted the development of a

collective sense of solidarity in the face of adversity.

The third significant stage of this social and political transformation came with the establishment of the Kurdish Regional Government and the acceptance of multiparty democracy and a relationship with the central government in Baghdad that allows considerable regional autonomy within a federal structure.

4

HISTORY

Dwelling since ancient times in the mountain ranges that rise between the modern-day states of Turkey, Iran, Iraq and Syria, the Kurds have always occupied a position of geographic importance in the Middle East. Their rocky terrain has been criss-crossed by foraging armies of the various great empires.

The Kurds were tragically overlooked in the great carving-up of Middle Eastern territory following the First World War. Subsequently, Kurds suffered varying degrees of oppression in each of the states in which they were to become a small but persistently valiant ethnic minority. It is only in recent years that the Kurds have succeeded in securing their own autonomous region – in north-western Iraq.

The saying goes that the Kurds have no friends but the mountains. A consolation might be that there is no shortage of them – tier upon tier of rugged rock have provided a safe and largely inaccessible haven for the Kurds since ancient times.

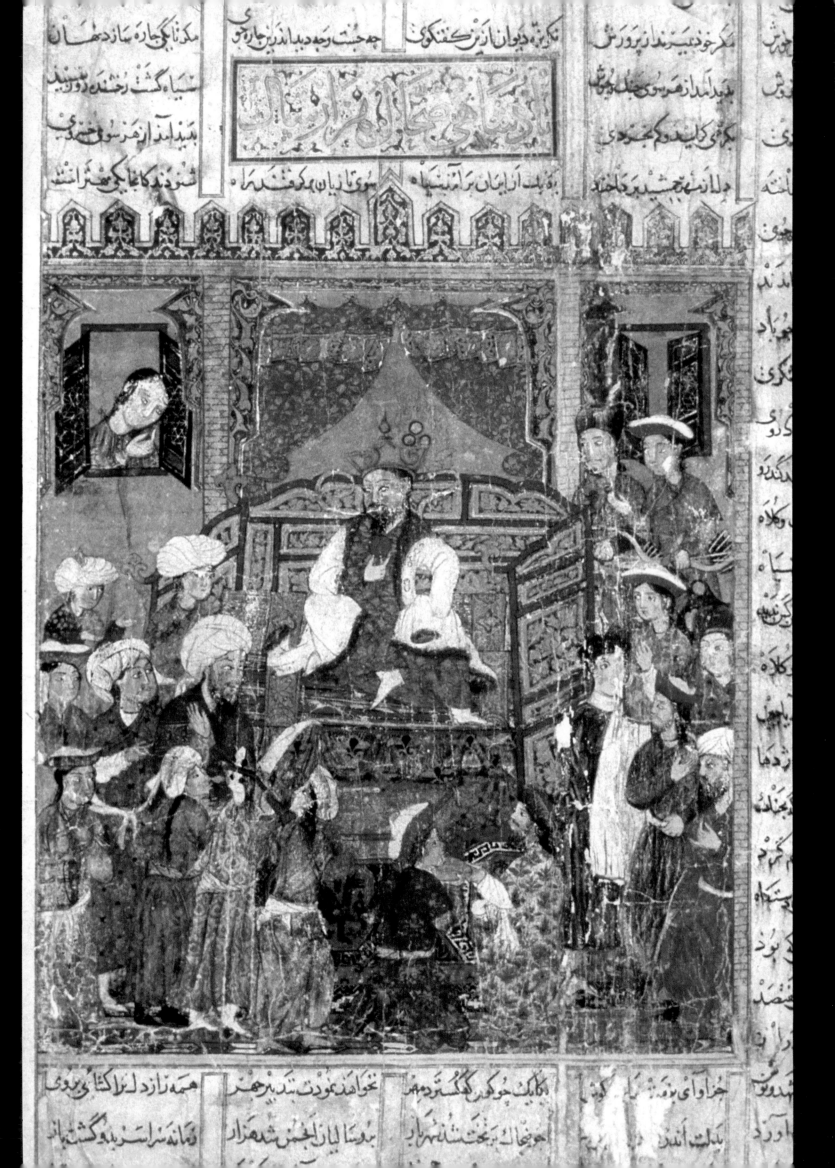

The Kurds claim, with probable justification, to be amongst the most long-settled peoples of the Middle East, though the lack of conclusive written evidence leaves room for considerable speculation. It seems likely that most people who today identify themselves as Kurds are the descendants of Indo–European tribes who moved into the Region in successive westward migrations more than three thousand years ago. To them must also be added people of Arab descent or of other origins, many of whom moved to the Region and over generations developed a Kurdish cultural identity. The first unequivocal reference to 'Cyrtii' comes from the second century BC, being applied to tribes dwelling in the Zagros Mountains, the largest range in modern Iran and Iraq. However, as one knowledgeable Western scholar of Kurdish history has noted, 'by the time of the Islamic conquests a thousand years later, and probably for some time before, the term Kurd had a socio-economic rather than [an] ethnic meaning. It was used of nomads on the western edge of the Iranian plateau and probably also of the tribes that acknowledged the Sassanians in Mesopotamia, many of which must have been Semitic.'

Over the centuries, there developed among these largely mountain-dwelling peoples a sense of difference, of 'otherness', when compared with the communities that surrounded them and from time to time invaded them. That sense of distinctiveness was reinforced by myths that were passed on from one generation to the next, as part of the Kurds' oral tradition. One such myth claims that the Kurds are descended from children who fled into the mountains in order to escape a child-eating giant, Zuhak. Another maintains that their ancestors were the progeny of slave girls from the court of King Solomon driven up into the mountains because they had been sired by a demon named Jasad. A common thread of being outcasts runs through these stories, as well as an almost mystical link to the mountainous terrain that the Kurds had made their own. From this homeland they could look defiantly on the peoples down below, as expressed vividly in the late

seventeenth century poem 'Mam-ou-Zeen', by the Kurdish poet and philosopher, Ahmad-e Khani:

Look, from the Arabs to the Georgians,
The Kurds have become like towers.
The Turks and Persians are surrounded
by them.
The Kurds are on all four corners.
Both sides have made the Kurdish people
Targets for the arrows of fate.
They are said to be keys to the borders
Each tribe forming a formidable bulwark.
Whenever the Ottoman Sea and Tajik Sea
Flow out and agitate,
The Kurds get soaked in blood
Separating them like an isthmus.

It is interesting to see the poet there likening the Turks and the Persians to seas. The Land of the Kurds – or 'Kurdistan' – was always viewed as landlocked, as well as predominantly mountainous, long before it acquired a defined geography. This landlocked state in itself inevitably limited the Kurds' contact with and knowledge of the outside world and helped generate suspicion or mistrust of the 'other'.

During many periods of Middle Eastern history that suspicion and mistrust was mutual. The culture of the nomadic Kurds, moving with their flocks of sheep and goats across hillside pastures, had little in common with their more sedentary neighbours, who developed major urban centres and a sophisticated literature. Early Kurdish settlements were predominantly much smaller villages. Between the seventh and ninth centuries AD, most of the Kurds converted to Islam and organised their society within an essentially feudal system, later modified in some cases by the evolution of religious brotherhoods. But significant numbers of people continued to follow other religious traditions, such as Christianity, Judaism and the Yezidi faith, with adherents of a variety of different religions often living alongside each other.

By the 1639 Treaty of Qasr-e Shirin, the rival Ottoman and Safavid empires brought an end to their territorial disputes and drew a frontier between themselves which ran through the Zagros Mountains. This division left a majority of the Kurds theoretically on the Ottoman side, though they were left pretty much to their own devices and continued to migrate largely at will. Meanwhile, their own civic organisation developed into a network of principalities; by the nineteenth century, there were 17 of these, nearly half of which had the right to mint their own currency. They enjoyed a considerable degree of autonomy until the Sublime Porte in Constantinople decided to establish a more substantial Ottoman presence, dividing the empire up into *vilayets* or provinces, of which six had a predominantly Kurdish population. Perhaps the most famous of the nineteenth century Kurdish princely leaders to stand up against Ottoman rule was Badr Khan, who declared the territory he ruled over to be independent. His army laid waste to neighbouring Nestorian communities, prompting loud protests from Britain and France, who demanded that Constantinople intervene to save the local Christian population. Ottoman forces finally laid siege to Badr Khan's fortress at Urukh until he surrendered in 1847

Above:
During the nineteenth century there was widespread opposition to Ottoman rule among the Kurdish populations of the Empire. This picture from 1880 shows members of the Bedirkhan family who were at the forefront of insurrectionary activities against the Ottoman government.

Right:
Western influence in Kurdistan increased greatly in the nineteenth century as colonial powers grew more interested in its strategic importance. Among those active in the Region were missionaries such as the American Dr Cochrane, shown here meeting with a Kurdish tribal chieftain circa 1880, most likely a comrade of Sheikh Obeidallah who played a key role leading the movement for recognition of a separate Kurdish identity.

Opposite:
In the 19th century much of the Middle East was ruled over by the Ottoman Empire (and to the east, Persia), a control that was increasingly no more than nominal as British and French colonial power strengthened. This late nineteenth century map takes little account of this power struggle but sketches an estimate of the ethnic group – Kurdistan was recognised as a large area.

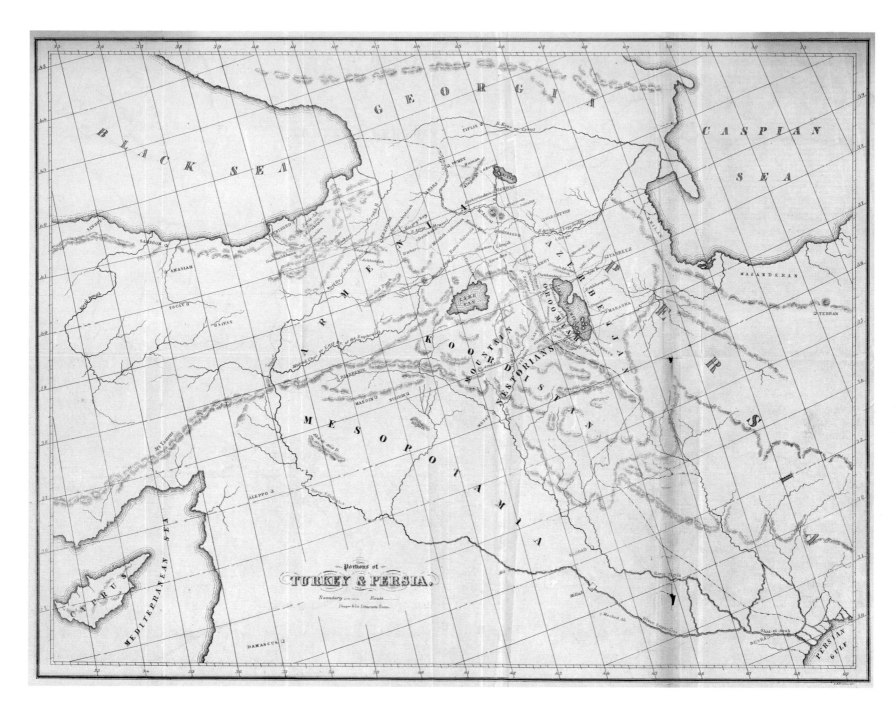

and was exiled to Crete. Despite the undoubted brutality of his military activities, he entered Kurdish folklore as one of the earliest proponents of Kurdish independence.

Another prominent figure in the development of Kurdish nationalism was Sheikh Obeidallah of Nahri, who led a military expedition into Persia in 1880, with the express purpose of establishing Kurdish autonomy. As he explained in a letter to British representatives in the Region, dated 5 October 1880, the Kurdish nation was 'a people apart. Their religion is different, and their laws and customs are distinct… The Chief and Rulers of Kurdistan, whether Turkish or Persian subjects, and the inhabitants of Kurdistan, one and all are united and agreed that matters cannot be carried on in this way with the two Governments, and that necessarily something must be done… We want our affairs to be in our own hands.' This clear plea for moral support, which was studied seriously in London, was somewhat undermined by the activities of Obeidallah and his son Muhammad Sadiq and their forces, many of whose men raided Persian territory and then retired to their mountain fastnesses with their booty. The British Consul General in Tabriz, William Abbott, met Obeidallah near Urumiya and reported back to London that he had asked the Sheikh whether his objective was to turn Kurdistan into a separate principality. 'To this the Sheikh replied that nobody ever doubted his loyalty to the Sultan, but that he had a very poor opinion of the local Pashas [officials].' Abbott's counterpart in Erzerum, Henry Trotter, came to the same conclusion, informing his Ambassador in Constantinople that he believed 'the Sheikh to be more or less

personally loyal to the Sultan; and he would be ready to submit to his authority and pay him tribute as long as he could get rid of the Ottoman officials, and be looked de jure as well as de facto the ruling chief of Kurdistan.' However, Obeidallah's ambitions were thwarted by military defeat and he was removed from Kurdistan to Constantinople. He succeeded in escaping to the Hejaz in Arabia in 1882, but died there the following year.

The Ottoman Empire had meanwhile been losing its European possessions; not for nothing was it increasingly referred to as 'the sick man of Europe'. This malaise led to a group of reformist nationalists, dubbed the Young Turks, to take effective control of affairs in Constantinople. As part of their modernisation programme aimed at dragging the Ottoman Empire into the twentieth century, they sought technical assistance from abroad, notably Germany, in matters such as railway construction. But in what would prove to be a fatal decision, they allied themselves to Germany and Austria–Hungary in the First World War, leading to a defeat that would bring about the dismemberment of the Empire, largely at the hands of the British and French, who had been plotting the expansion of their spheres of influence in the Middle East long before the guns stopped firing. The Kurdish Ottoman provinces, however, resisted the Allied advances. Not one of the main urban centres of the predominantly Kurdish *vilayets* was occupied by Allied forces until after the Moudros Armistice of 31 October 1918. British troops entered Mosul on 7 November and, four weeks later, Georges Clemenceau ceded France's rights over the Mosul *vilayet*, with the proviso that his country could enjoy a share of the region's oil. Suleimaniah, in contrast, remained in Kurdish hands.

The question now was what would happen to the Kurdish areas of the former Ottoman Empire. The messages coming out of London and Paris were far from clear, but, unabashed, General Sherif Pasha Khandan of Suleimaniah – a former Ottoman ambassador to Sweden – arrived at the Versailles Peace Conference in January 1919 with a map of what he called Great Kurdistan, stretching from the Mediterranean Sea to the Persian Gulf. Two months later, the Kurdish delegation to the peace conference submitted a memorandum calling for Kurdish independence and the

Opposite:
With the collapse of the Ottoman Empire new states emerged in the region. The borders of Turkey, Syria and Iraq were all established taking little account of the sort of ethnic dispersal sketched in the late nineteenth century map on the previous page. Modern-day Iraqi Kurdistan fell under the British Mandate of 1920.

Right:
The most important leader of the early Kurdish nationalist movement was Mulla Mustafa Barzani. He can be seen here seated third from left, with his men in Shaqlawa, Iraq.

bringing together of all Kurds within a sovereign state.

The international community was not entirely hostile to this idea. The US President, Woodrow Wilson, had declared in the twelfth of his famous Fourteen Points that the non-Turkish minorities of the Ottoman Empire should be granted the right of 'autonomous development'. Moreover, Articles 62 and 64 of the Treaty of Sèvres (1920) provided for 'local autonomy' for predominantly Kurdish areas, admitting the possibility that the 'Kurdish peoples' might one day be granted 'independence' from Turkey. Turkey was struggling to construct a new nation state based on Anatolia and a relatively small foothold in the Balkans, while repulsing Greek ambitions towards its territory. They hoped to gain control of Mosul, but the rest of the Kurdish areas they had given up as lost. However, the British, who had been granted a mandate by the League of Nations over Mesopotamia and were busy creating the new country of Iraq, were determined not to lose Mosul *vilayet*, not just for their own commercial interests, but also because they feared that Iraq could not be a viable state without that region's oil.

Nonetheless, London continued to accept in principle that the Kurds deserved some degree of self-rule. In a joint Anglo–Iraqi declaration to the Council of the League of Nations on 24 December 1922, for example, it was stated that, 'His Majesty's Government and the government of Iraq recognise the rights of the Kurds who live within the frontiers of Iraq to establish a Government within those frontiers. Our two Governments hope that the various Kurdish groups will reach some mutual agreement as quickly as possible as to the form they wish this Government to take and as to the boundaries within which they wish to extend its authority.'

The reference to 'various Kurdish groups' was significant. The variegated affiliations and aspirations among Kurds even within the boundaries of Iraq would often act as an impediment to a coherent strategy for gaining regional autonomy, let alone any form of statehood. It must be said, of course, that whatever favourable noises were made by Britain or other outside powers, none of Kurdistan's neighbours relished the idea of an independent Kurdish state, least of all Turkey or Persia (which changed its name to Iran in 1935).

Iraq itself, both before and after its formal independence in 1932, was very wary of any Kurdish aspirations that might question the new country's territorial integrity. Only in 1926 had the Council of the League of Nations recognised the incorporation of Mosul into Iraq. At that time, however, the League proclaimed through an International Commission of Inquiry, that 'the desire of the Kurds that the administrators, magistrates and teachers in their country be drawn from their own ranks, and adopt Kurdish as the official language in all their activities, will be taken into account.' Ominously, despite the adoption in Baghdad of a Local Languages Law, the provisions set out in the League of Nations recommendation were not incorporated into the Anglo–Iraqi Treaty of 1930, which formed the basis for Iraq's independence.

The spectre of separatism and the threat of resultant regional instability loomed in both Baghdad and London. These fears were not without foundation, though the Kurds in the period after the First World War were seriously divided over what they really wanted, and some developments since the Versailles Peace Conference had weakened British and Iraqi confidence in the Kurdish partners with whom

they were dealing. Sheikh Mahmoud Barzanji of Suleimaniah was a notable case in point. In 1919, the British invited him to act as Governor there, believing he would be useful in keeping the Kurds onside while they constructed Iraq. But the Sheikh secretly put out feelers to the Turks and even more dramatically declared himself the King of Kurdistan. This was an obvious slap in the face to the Hashemite Faisal, who the British were setting up to occupy the throne in Baghdad, following his ignominious ousting from Damascus by the French. 'King' Mahmoud of Kurdistan was a thorn in the side of the British and the Baghdad authorities for several years, and when it was deemed necessary, the British deployed the Royal Air Force to bomb his troops, thereby suppressing any uprising before it might become too dangerous. He was finally defeated only in the spring of 1931.

In the meantime, the nature of Kurdish society was changing and new facets of what one might call Kurdish nationalism were appearing. This was partly because of a degree of urbanisation, which brought with it greater literacy and a certain politicisation of tribal and religious communities. In September 1930, there were strikes and demonstrations in

Suleimaniah as people asserted their desire for change. New leaders gained prominence, not least Mulla Mustafa Barzani of the Barzani tribe (from Barzan), which acquired tremendous status amongst many Kurds, especially amongst followers of the Naqshbandi Sufi Order. Though the Barzanis were a smaller tribe than some of their traditional enemies, such as the Zebaris and the Herkis, numbering only about 1,800 families or 9,000 people as late as 1945, they became the dominant force in Kurdish nationalism and remain important to this day. This is largely thanks to the legacy of Mulla Mustafa.

In contrast to many of his contemporaries, Mulla Mustafa was political from an early age. His father died in 1903, when Mulla Mustafa was only about four years old, and his elder brother, Sheikh Abd al-Salam II (who had inherited the mantle of religious leadership that had fallen on his family), was hanged by the Ottomans six years later for opposing new laws brought in by the Young Turks. As a tiny infant, Mulla Mustafa spent time in prison himself along with his mother. As a young man, he was obliged by the authorities to live in Suleimaniah, where he spent much time in religious studies, becoming a noted Qur'anic expert as well as improving his knowledge of the arts of politics and statecraft. He was an imposing figure, powerfully built, and made a strong impression on the foreigners he met. The US Ambassador to Iraq, William Eagleton Jnr, observed that Barzani 'quickly grasped the essence of a situation and exercised diplomatic and military cunning in achieving his objective,' though he added less flatteringly, 'less commendable characteristics were Mulla Mustafa's egotism, opportunism, short-sightedness and vulnerability.'

In 1943, Mulla Mustafa (whose first name, incidentally, does not have an overtly religious connotation) was able to leave Suleimaniah and return to Barzan, where he started to build new alliances and finesse his aspirations for the future of the Kurds. Iraqi Prime Minister Nuri al-Said dispatched a provincial governor, Majid Mustafa, himself a Kurd, to Barzan to get a

Opposite:
Mulla Mustafa Barzani is revered as one of the founding fathers of modern Kurdistan, and is a nationalist hero. This portrait, hanging in the new parliament building in Erbil, is flanked by a ceremonial guard in traditional dress.

Right:
As part of the public effort to honour him in the nation's collective cultural memory, Mustafa Barzani is portrayed widely in images. This cast for a new sculpture created in a workshop in Suleimaniah will serve to create yet another tribute to the celebrated Kurdish hero.

clearer idea of Barzani's demands. These included the delineation of a Kurdish province comprising the districts of Kirkuk, Suleimaniah, Erbil, Dohuk and Khanaqin, which would enjoy cultural, economic and agricultural autonomy. All internal matters, other than those concerning the army and gendarmerie, would be placed under the authority of a discrete Minister for Kurdish Affairs within the Iraqi Cabinet. The Kurdish language would be recognised as an official language and be taught in schools, as in principle it was meant to have been since 1932. Barzani even went to Baghdad to press his case, but there were many within the Iraqi government who feared that to accede would inevitably lead to Kurdish separatism. Nuri al-Said was forced to resign in June 1944, and Majid Mustafa was dismissed. Disappointed by this failure, Barzani decided to concentrate on military action instead.

At first Barzani's forces enjoyed some success, but ultimately they could not withstand the superior might of the Iraqi army, supplemented by the support of loyalist Kurdish tribes such as the Zebaris. Barzani was obliged to retreat over the frontier into Iran, accompanied by several thousand of his tribesmen. The situation in Iran, meanwhile, had given rise to some interesting new developments. During the Second World War, the Soviet Union and Britain – unlikely but inevitable allies in the war against fascism – maintained a large presence in Iran, in an effort to keep the Germans out. The Russians gave support to an Iranian Kurd by the name of Qazi Muhammad, who took advantage of immediate post-war uncertainties in January 1946 to declare an independent state in Iranian Kurdistan, which became known as the Mahabad Republic. Mulla Mustafa Barzani made his way there and, after overcoming initial suspicion from the Iranian Kurds, became an important figure in the short-lived statelet. There was no way that the government in Tehran would tolerate the Mahabad Republic's existence for long, however, and before the end of the year it had been suppressed. Barzani and his followers sought refuge in the mountains on the Iran–Iraq border, before making an epic overland journey to the Soviet Union. This has sometimes been compared to the Communist Chinese Long March, though Barzani's trek lasted only 52 days, not many months.

The Russians were initially wary of Barzani and his followers, sending them to live in different parts of the Soviet Union. Barzani himself spent time in Baku (Azerbaijan), Tashkent (Uzbekistan) and Yerevan (Armenia), from where he was sometimes able to make radio broadcasts beamed at Iraq. He spent most of his time improving his education, however, learning Russian and studying previously unfamiliar subjects such as Economics and Science. This obviously involved coming to terms with the Soviet Union's dominant Marxist–Leninist ideology. However, despite more than a decade in the USSR – the latter part in Moscow – he never became a Communist. His long association with the Soviet Union nonetheless made him and to an extent the whole Kurdish nationalist movement suspect in Western eyes, particularly after the Cold War set in.

In July 1958, there was a bloody *coup d'état* in Baghdad, which overthrew the Hashemite monarchy. Iraq's new leader was General Abdul

Karim Qassem, who invited Barzani back to be a part of the new order. He was even allocated the grand residence in which former Prime Minister Nuri al-Said had once lived. General Qassem legalised Barzani's Kurdish Democratic Party (KDP) and authorised the publication of a range of Kurdish-language media. Even more significant, the new provisional constitution of 27 July 1958 declared that 'the Kurds and the Arabs are partners within this nation. The constitution guarantees their rights within the framework of the Iraqi Republic.'

Enthused by the seemingly benign nature of the new regime, Mulla Mustafa Barzani worked closely with the government, even sending some of his men to put down a revolt among Iraqi soldiers in Mosul in March 1959. But he became less enamoured of the Baghdad government as the months went by and he realised that the Kurds were not going to be given the degree of self-rule he had imagined. In July 1961, he presented a petition to General Qassem demanding full Kurdish autonomy within an essentially federal state. According to Barzani's blueprint, foreign affairs and defence would remain the responsibility of the government in Baghdad, along with national economic policy, but the government of the Kurdish autonomous region would expect to

control such portfolios as education, health, communications, municipal and rural affairs within its territory. The demands did not stop there. Barzani and the KDP wanted a Kurd to be Vice-President, along with all the assistant Ministers in the federal ministry. Finally, Kurdish army units could only be deployed by the national government with the consent of Kurdish political leaders. This was a step too far in the eyes of General Qassem, who rejected the petition. As an official government explanation put it, 'The concessions which the Kurds of Iraq under Mulla Mustafa's leadership demand are out of proportion with their number in this country, the area of land inhabited by them or the contribution made by them as a community to the national output.'

This put-down by Baghdad helped align some of the Kurdish tribes who previously had been ill-disposed to Barzani. He was now able to return to his homeland, his honour intact, and start an armed revolt against the Iraqi government. His fighting men expelled some of the Iraqi security forces from installations in Kurdistan and, when the Iraqi Air Force bombed Barzan in September 1961, leading to many civilian casualties, more of the local population rallied to Mulla Mustafa's banner in their outrage. The Kurdish Peshmergas (those

Above:
Sheikh Mahmoud Hafid, who played a central role in the Republic's creation, is commemorated by a painting in the main square of Suleimaniah, a town which he had announced as capital of the earlier state of Kurdistan declared in 1922.

Left:
The short-lived Mahabad Republic was a brave and daring effort to create a Kurdish homeland. The archive photograph shows the cabinet and other officials, along with their leader Qazi Muhammad who is seated at the front. He was to be hanged by the Iranian authorities on 31 March 1947.

Above:
Four officers who bravely stood by Qazi Muhammad were also executed, commemorated here in a statue that stands next to the central park in Suleimaniah today. Mustafa Barzani, who had been appointed General in the breakaway republic, embarked on a long march northwards, accompanied by a band of loyal followers, and finally found sanctuary in Soviet Russia.

who willingly face death) were able to harass Iraqi forces who tried to seize rebel territory. They knew the territory intimately and rather like T.E. Lawrence's Bedouin fighters in Arabia half a century before could strike quickly and then simply melt away.

In February 1963, General Qassem was overthrown by the Ba'ath Party, which launched a major offensive against the Kurdish forces four months later. Although the Ba'ath Party fell from power after only nine months in government, its successors continued to espouse a military approach to the Iraqi Kurdish question.

In the meantime, the Kurdish Democratic Party was afflicted by serious schisms, with Barzani himself coming under fire from some critics for allegedly being a 'tribal chief' and 'a

rightist'. There is reason to believe that SAVAK, the Shah of Iran's notorious secret police, deliberately fomented these divisions which reached such a serious state that the KDP's Secretary General, Ibrahim Ahmed, used a broadcast on the Kurdish radio station Denge Kurdistan, in July 1964, to call on the Peshmergas to revolt against Barzani. However, this attempted putsch within the movement was thwarted and Ibrahim Ahmed was forced to seek sanctuary in Iran along with a few hundred of his supporters. Amongst these was his son-in-law Jalal Talabani, who decided to return to Iraq the following year. Unable to patch up his differences with the mainstream of the KDP, he went over to the other side, aiding the Iraqi government in its campaign against the Kurdish uprising.

There was a renewed offensive in June 1966, against which Barzani's Peshmergas scored some notable victories, which prompted the then Iraqi Prime Minister, Abdul Rahman Aref, to draft the so-called 29 June Declaration, which recognised Kurdish national rights and proposed a substantial degree of devolved power. Mulla Mustafa Barzani happily accepted this as the basis for negotiations of a settlement to the conflict, but Iraqi army chiefs were horrified and demanded its withdrawal. The

on a new offensive. Yet, despite its use of aircraft and heavy artillery, the Iraqi army was unable to break through the Peshmerga defences and it was clear that this stalemate would not be resolved by force. Accordingly, the Ba'ath Party passed at its seventh Congress in 1969 a resolution which could in principle form the basis of a peaceful solution. As well as recognising the Kurdish nation as such, the resolution included several specific measures such as approval for Kurdish–language

Left:
In 1966, the then Iraqi Prime Minister Abdul Rahman Aref realized that concessions for the Kurds would be better than continued conflict. During a visit to northern Iraq he met with Mustafa Barzani and appealed to rebelling Kurdish tribesmen to cooperate with Iraqi Arabs in order to preserve the unity of the country.

Opposite:
The peace treaty signed in 1970 by Mustafa Barzani and Saddam Hussein when they met gave considerable rights to the Kurdish population in Iraq and new levels of autonomy in areas such as education and cultural expression.

Aref government never really recovered from this setback and on 17 July 1968 the Ba'ath Party carried out another coup which would keep them in power in Baghdad for the next 35 years. Though the first Ba'ath President was General Ahmed Hassan al-Bakr, the real power behind the throne – who would later formally occupy it himself – was a younger and far more ruthless man, Saddam Hussein.

The new Ba'ath administration was keen to put out feelers to the KDP to reach some peaceful settlement of the conflict, but once again military leaders were opposed and insisted

teaching, the establishment of a university at Suleimaniah and permission for the publication of Kurdish–language media. Saddam Hussein then went personally to meet Mustafa Barzani at his headquarters near Haj Omran to persuade him to accept the offer of a peace agreement which would accord considerable autonomy to Kurdistan. The exact geographical delimitation of this proposed autonomous region, as well as issues relating to the region's substantial oil reserves, could be discussed over a four-year transition period. Though Barzani came under strong pressure from the Shah of

Iran to reject this offer, the Soviet Union and other friendly outside powers urged him to accept and it seemed too good an opportunity to let pass.

Accordingly, on 11 March 1970, President Ahmed Hassan al-Bakr went on national television to announce a 15-point manifesto which was designed to bring about national reconciliation by offering the Kurds more than most would have dreamed possible. The Kurdish language would be granted equal status with Arabic in areas that had a majority Kurdish population and would be taught elsewhere in Iraq as a second language within the limits prescribed by the law. All discrimination against Kurds and other nationals in regard to holding public office, including Cabinet ministries and senior army commands, would be removed. A plan would be worked out in regard to the language and cultural rights of the Kurdish people, including building more schools in the Kurdish areas, elevating the standards of education and admitting, at a fair rate, Kurdish students to universities and military colleges and granting them scholarships. In the administrative units populated by a Kurdish majority, government officials would be appointed from among Kurds or persons well versed in the Kurdish language: the governor, director of police and other principal government functionaries should be Kurds.

Furthermore, the government recognised the right of the Kurdish people to set up student, youth, women's and teachers' organisations. Workers, government functionaries and employees – civilian and military – who had been involved in the recent conflict should be allowed back into service. A committee of specialists, under the Ministry of Northern Affairs, would be established to speed up the development of the Kurdish areas, as well as providing indemnities for the afflictions of past years. An economic plan would be drawn up in such a way as to ensure equal progress for the various parts of Iraq, with due attention paid to the backward condition of the Kurdish areas. Pensions should be granted to the families of members of the Kurdish armed movements

who had been killed in the hostilities, as well as to those who had been incapacitated or disfigured.

The inhabitants of both Arab and Kurdish villages would be repatriated to their original place of habitation. Citizens whose villages lay in areas that had been requisitioned by the government for public utility purposes would be settled in neighbouring districts and compensated for any loss incurred. The implementation of the Agrarian Reform Law in

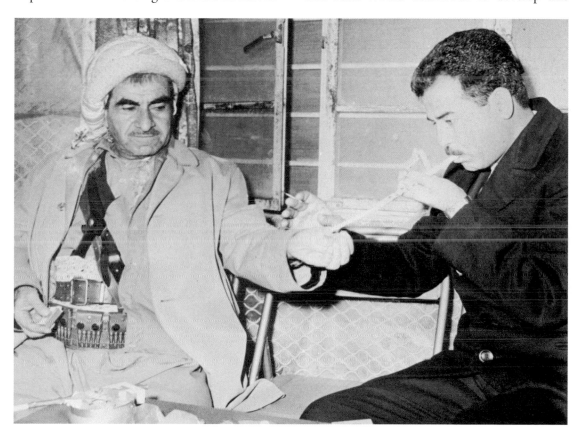

Kurdish areas would be accelerated and that Law should be amended so as to liquidate all feudalistic relationships, handing out plots to all peasants and waiving their agricultural tax arrears relating to the period of conflict.

Most significantly, the Ba'athist Interim Constitution of Iraq would be amended to acknowledge that the people of Iraq are composed of two principal nationalities: the Arab nationality and the Kurdish nationality. That Constitution would recognise the national rights of the Kurdish people and the rights of all nationalities within the framework of Iraqi

unity. A paragraph would be added to Article 4 of the Constitution, viz: 'The Kurdish language shall be, besides the Arabic language, an official language in the Kurdish area.' One of the Vice-Presidents of the Republic would be a Kurd.

Finally, following the publication of this manifesto, necessary steps were to be taken to unify the governorates and administrative units populated by a Kurdish majority as shown by an official census, which would be carried out. The State would endeavour to develop this administrative unity and both deepen and broaden the Kurdish people's process of exercising their national rights as a measure of self-rule. Pending the realisation of administrative unity, Kurdish national affairs would be coordinated by means of periodical meetings between the High Committee and the governors of the northern area.

As self-rule was to be established within the framework of the Republic of Iraq, the exploitation of the natural riches in the area would nonetheless be the prerogative of the authorities of the Republic. However, the

Kurdish people would contribute to the legislative power in proportion to their share of the population of Iraq.

To most Kurds, battered by years of military assaults and long constrained by all sorts of restrictions due to their ethnicity and linguistic status, this all seemed too good to be true. And so, alas, in the short term it proved to be, though this manifesto would serve as a sort of template for future agreements. For a brief honeymoon period, however, all went well between the Ba'athist government and the KDP. Vice-President Saddam Hussein and several other government figures stood on a balcony in Baghdad alongside two of Mulla Mustafa Barzani's sons, Idris and Masoud, and other Kurdish representatives, waving at a cheering crowd celebrating the apparent resolution of the

country's Kurdish question. Saddam Hussein was determined to milk the opportunity to claim the maximum personal credit for this breakthrough.

However, problems soon emerged within the High Committee comprising Ba'athist and Kurdish representatives, charged with implementing the agreement. There were disputes about the precise geographic delineation of the Kurdish autonomous region, most notably over the question of whether the Kirkuk district, so richly endowed with oil, would form part of it. Meanwhile, as the Kurds protested, the Baghdad government was moving Arab settlers into Kirkuk in an effort to Arabise it – a complaint bitterly reiterated by Kurds over the succeeding years. More blatantly, when the provisional Iraqi

constitution was issued in July 1970 it did not, as had been promised, include the amendments concerning the national rights of the Kurdish people. The Kurds protested when 40,000 Shi'ite Kurds who had lived for generations in Baghdad and other areas outside the designated Kurdish Region were expelled in an exercise of ethnic cleansing. There were assassination attempts against Mulla Mustafa Barzani and his son Idris. The Kurds suspected this was the work of Saddam Hussein, who was already acquiring a reputation for murderous ruthlessness in his gradual accumulation, and later maintenance, of absolute power within Iraq. For its part, the government issued a long list of complaints against the Kurds for alleged breaches of the agreement and bad faith, including the accusation that Barzani and his colleagues were in cahoots with Iran, and that their real aim was to achieve sovereign independence for Kurdistan.

The extent of the Ba'athists' backtracking on the March 1970 Manifesto became clear in March 1974, when the government issued a new Autonomy Law, which fell far short of the earlier pledges. Almost immediately, the civil war was reignited. An estimated 100,000 Kurds, including many officials and intellectuals as well as an enthusiastic young corps of volunteer fighters, left Baghdad and other cities and towns across Iraq to join the 'Revolution' in the north. For a while, the Kurdish army was well stocked with supplies from Iran, which enabled it – along with its renewed use of guerrilla tactics – to hold its own against the numerically superior Iraqi national army. But on 6 March 1975, in Algiers, the Shah of Iran signed an agreement with the Baghdad government, according to which Iran would end its support to the Iraqi Kurds in return for increased access to the Shatt-al-Arab River and the transfer of a small area of territory to Iran.

Within months, the Kurdish forces had to throw in the towel. Nearly 180,000 of them moved to Iran, while over 200,000 handed themselves over to the government side and were deported to the south of the country, where many died from disease, unsanitary living conditions and unfamiliarity with the climate. Mulla Mustafa Barzani, dejected and feeling his age due to the onset of cancer, went into exile, first in Tehran and then in the United States, where he settled in Alexandria, Virginia. He died on 1 March 1979, largely forgotten by the world apart from those Kurds for whom he would always remain a great hero. The recent overthrow of the Shah and the Iranian Islamic Revolution had given him hope that he might be able to go back home, but the opportunity had come too late. Eventually, the legacy of his nationalistic struggle would pass to his sons, most notably Idris and Masoud. Idris led the KDP in exile, from Iran, until his death of natural causes in 1987. Masoud is the current President of the KDP and has been elected President of the Kurdistan Region.

After a period of acute demoralisation, the KDP regrouped itself as an organisation, notably among young exiles based in Europe. Part of the new enthusiasm resulted from the Kurds' fierce opposition to Saddam Hussein, who had ousted his cousin Ahmed Hassan al-Bakr from the Iraqi presidency on 17 July 1979.

But another important factor was the growing rivalry between the KDP and the Patriotic Union of Kurdistan (PUK), led by Mulla Mustafa Barzani's old adversary, Jalal Talabani. The PUK was essentially Marxist–Leninist in orientation and had been formed in the wake of the Algiers Accords, with the backing of the government in Syria. PUK literature denounced what it called the reactionary and tribal leadership of the Barzanis and clearly outlined its animosity towards the KDP in general. The two main Kurdish nationalist groups spent considerable energy fighting each other rather than concentrating their ire against Baghdad.

On 17 September 1980 Saddam Hussein went on television to condemn what he said were numerous outrages by the Iranian regime, before melodramatically ripping up the Algiers Accords. Five days later, Iraqi troops crossed the frontier into Iran, triggering a war – known in the region as the First Gulf War – that would last nearly a decade and cost millions of young lives. The Iraqi state coffers were full, thanks to oil revenues, and the army was well equipped with modern hardware supplied by France, Britain, and the Soviet Union and other outside powers happy with the idea that the upstart Islamic Republic of Iran might be hobbled in

its infancy. After initial Iraqi successes, the advantage moved more towards the Iranian side, its army inflamed by Ayatollah Khomeini's energetic speeches and promises of religious martyrdom. Iran is predominantly composed of Shi'ite Muslims, and Shi'ites constitute the largest religious group inside Iraq, although Saddam Hussein gave a privileged position during his years in power to Arab Sunnis.

Meanwhile, Saddam Hussein set about expelling or purging sections of Iraq's own population. In 1980, a decree was issued calling for the expulsion of all inhabitants of Safavid (Persian Shi'ite) descent and the expropriation of their assets. A high proportion of the people affected were Shi'ite Kurds, living mainly in Baghdad and the south of Iraq. Several thousand young Shi'ite Kurds were accordingly rounded up and disappeared; they were almost certainly killed. Similarly, in 1983, several thousand more Kurds were arrested, on the pretext that they were originally from the Barzan area of Kurdistan and therefore unreliable. Their eventual fate was only discovered when mass graves containing their bodies were found after the US-led intervention in Iraq in 2003.

In 1984, Saddam Hussein ordered the

The giant monument to those who perished in Halabja in 1988 under three days of chemical bombing stands outside the town in well-tended gardens (*opposite above*). The names of the 5,000 people who died are inscribed in marble (*above left*) around the central chamber, divided into families and listed alphabetically. The atrocities were recorded by the Irananian photographer Ozuturk who arrived with Iranian crews at the site of the massacre some three days later. These are displayed in the high atrium (*above*) which opens into the museum rooms, a site visited by mourners and sympathisers from across the world.

Overleaf:
The named graves of the 5,000 who died in the Halabja massacres are laid out in orderly rows in a peaceful cemetery not from the site of the Monument to the Martyrs of Halabja.

systematic destruction of villages in Kurdistan and the deportation of their inhabitants into what were essentially concentration camps. The situation deteriorated further in 1987, when one of the President's cousins, Ali Hassan al-Majid (later nicknamed Chemical Ali, for deployment of chemical weapons) was given the responsibility of bringing Kurdistan to heel. A census was taken in Kirkuk and other towns and only those who figured on the list or who were housed in the concentration camps would be entitled to receive food rations. Anyone outside these limited areas was considered fair game for the security and armed forces. Vast areas of Kurdistan were to be emptied of all living things, including animals. All signs of life or civilisation were to be wiped out. Thus began what became known as the Anfal Campaign – the attempted genocide of a people by the government of a country of which in principle they were citizens. An estimated 180,000 Kurds died in the Anfal Campaign, as a result of bombardments, chemical weapons, being held in inhuman conditions or being transported to the south of Iraq. Tens of thousands did manage to escape to Iran or Turkey, but they were a fortunate minority.

The atrocities being carried out against Iraq's Kurds were brought to the world's attention by media coverage of the results of chemical-weapons attacks by the Iraqi Air Force on the Kurdish town of Halabja on 16 March 1988. The town had just been taken by PUK Peshmerga and Iranian forces. The civilian population was defenceless. Men, women and children dropped dead in the street or suffocated in places where they had taken shelter. Over 5,000 men, women and children died instantly, and several thousand more perished over the following days. It was one of the worst crimes against humanity in modern history.

But Saddam Hussein had no scruples regarding the methods used in the Anfal Campaign. For him, the results were satisfactory, as within six months, government forces had complete control of Kurdistan.

Despite increasing evidence of the inhumanity of the regime in Baghdad, Iraq continued to receive military and economic assistance throughout the 1980s from a wide range of countries in the East and the West. The Iraqi war with Iran had dragged on senselessly, the carnage as dreadful and futile as that on the battlefields of Flanders in the First World War. It was finally brought to an end, with no tangible advantage to either side.

Saddam Hussein had created an image of himself as the guardian of the Arab world against the new Iranian revolution. However, on 22 August 1990, Iraqi troops moved into Kuwait and rapidly occupied the small Arab state. At various times since Iraq's birth as an independent state its government had looked enviously at the wealth of its much smaller neighbour. Now Saddam Hussein was trying to annex Kuwait, claiming that in reality it was an Iraqi province that needed to be brought back into the fold. The invasion was a clear violation of international law, and, after several unsuccessful diplomatic attempts to persuade the Iraqis to withdraw, the United States led a wide United-Nations-sanctioned coalition of both Western and Arab countries to force them out. Aerial bombing of Baghdad and other targets by Operation Desert Storm began on 17 January 1991 before ground forces entered. Resistance from the Iraqi forces proved to be nowhere near as fierce as had been expected, but vindictively the departing occupiers not only ransacked Kuwait City and carried off as much booty as they could, but also set fire to hundreds of Kuwait's oil wells.

George Bush Sr was President of the United States at the time. In a decision that is still a topic of great controversy, he agreed to a ceasefire on 27 February and halted the Allied advance on Baghdad. Even though loyalist forces might have fought hard to defend the Iraqi capital, leading to high numbers of casualties, toppling Saddam Hussein could have been a real possibility. But Washington seems to have feared the likely repercussions on regional security in such a case – not least, possible Iranian military incursions and uncertainty in Baghdad. Even Saddam Hussein seemed better than total chaos or a power vacuum. But the sudden ending of the Gulf War came as a bitter blow both to the Kurds of northern Iraq and some Shia contingents in the south. Both groups had been encouraged by the Americans to rise up against the Ba'athist government, but had then, as they saw it, been abandoned to suffer the consequences alone. The reprisals were indeed terrible. Saddam

Hussein pressed ahead with the draining of the southern marshlands, destroying the livelihood of the venerable Marsh Arabs, while in the north the government turned its full power against a Kurdish insurrection.

The insurrection at first brought important victories. Suleimaniah was taken by the Kurds on 7 March, followed by Erbil and Dohuk over the next few days. Kirkuk was the next targeted location, but the Iraqi Air Force then struck back and the tide was turned. The attacks were merciless, and, as refugees started to pour out of the towns in the hope of escaping the bombardments and ideally of reaching sanctuary in Turkey or Iran, they often found themselves being strafed from the air. Up to four million refugees took to the hills, where many died of cold, hunger, illness and fatigue, as well as from Iraqi military action. Alarmed by the scale of the possible influx of desperate refugees, Turkey and Iran closed their borders. The Kurds' plight became an issue of international concern, with the French spearheading efforts to get not only humanitarian aid into the region but also to mobilise the international community to act.

Since the founding of the United Nations towards the end of the Second World War, a central principle of the relations between nations had been that of non-interference in the internal affairs of a sovereign state. But the argument for humanitarian intervention in the case of Iraq's Kurds prompted action from three major powers.

The fact that there were large numbers of foreign troops in the vicinity facilitated rapid action once the decision had been taken. US and British ground troops went into Kurdistan from Turkey and a 'no-fly zone' was declared north of the 36th parallel and enforced by the US, British and French, which meant that Iraqi planes could not attack or harass the population north of that parallel. This still left Mosul and Suleimaniah theoretically unprotected, though eventually the no-fly zone was extended further south.

In the face of this new crisis, the two main Kurdish political forces, the KDP and the PUK,

set aside their bitter differences and formed a common Front with six other, smaller political groups. Strange as it may now seem, a delegation from this Kurdish Front, led by Jalal Talabani, went to Baghdad to negotiate with Saddam Hussein. He gave them a superficially warm welcome and agreed that Iraqi officials would be withdrawn from large areas of Kurdistan. From the Iraqi government's point of view, this had the advantage of enabling them to concentrate on their anti-dissident activity elsewhere in Iraq. Saddam Hussein and his army generals probably realised they could not win a war of attrition with the Kurds under the changed circumstances, so it was better to come to some sort of accommodation. Thus, by November 1991, the Front was in charge of a sizeable, non-productive, largely urban population in the north. Over the Kurdistan Region as a whole, there was general devastation. Approximately 90 per cent of the agricultural land had been laid to waste and around 4,500 out of 5,000 villages had been razed. As the Iraqi government was now operating a kind of blockade against the Region, supplies of both food and fuel were low. Large areas of forest were damaged as people scavenged for firewood. Unemployment was gauged at around 70 per cent and the average wage for a civil servant was just US$3 a month.

Despite these unpropitious circumstances, the Kurds were determined to press ahead with introducing democracy to the region. Elections were held in 1992, under a system of proportional representation. A minimum threshold of seven per cent was set for representation, which meant that very few parties other than the KDP and the PUK would win parliamentary seats. The two main parties were very evenly matched, and the principle of a fifty-fifty share of administrative posts was agreed. Nonetheless, tensions broke out between the KDP and the PUK in May 1994. Despite pleas from outside powers for the Kurds to remain calm, there was intermittent fighting between the rivals. The Kurdish Parliament building was even occupied for a

short while. President François Mitterrand of France invited the Kurdish leaders to Rambouillet for talks aimed at restoring cooperation, but they were unable to return to France later to sign the agreement, as Turkey refused to let them cross its land border.

In January 1995, Jalal Talabani ordered the mobilisation of his supporters and called for the KDP to be chased out of Kurdistan. What occurred on the ground, however, was that the Region had effectively been split into two zones of control, with the KDP holding sway in the north and west and the PUK in the south and east. At this point the United States tried to mediate, organising two rounds of talks at Drogheda in Ireland. Tensions between the two groups nonetheless continued and in August 1996 the Iranians gave assistance to a PUK offensive. Meanwhile, the KDP was receiving material supplies of all kinds through the frontier with Turkey, while the PUK got its supplies through the border with Iran. It was seen to be in the interest of both Turkey and Iran, not to mention Baghdad, that Kurdistan was so divided. The last thing any of them wanted at that time was a strong, united and autonomous Kurdistan Region.

The wider international community looked on with a mixture of sympathy and dismay. As Kurdistan was still part of Iraq, despite having in 1992 unilaterally declared its autonomy under a putative federal system, it was subject to UN sanctions applied against Saddam Hussein's regime. Nonetheless, a number of UN agencies worked in the region, as did a wide range of European and North American NGOs, including an educational foundation run by François Mitterrand's wife Danielle, who became so deeply involved in Kurdish issues that she acquired the sobriquet 'The Mother of the Kurds'. The British NGO MAG worked in helping clear an estimated 15 million landmines from Kurdistan's territory.

In the wake of the 9/11 attacks on New York and Washington and the Allied operation to topple the Taliban in Afghanistan, the United States began to apply pressure to the KDP and the PUK to get together and start planning what they would do if and when military action was taken against Saddam Hussein. When the predominantly American and British forces launched Operation Iraqi Freedom in March 2003, there was an outcry in much of the world, but Iraq's Kurds were unsurprisingly delighted. It was not just that they had every reason to despise this brutal dictator, who had been directly responsible for thousands of Kurdish deaths. He had also lied to them and betrayed their quest to achieve genuine autonomy within a federal system. The toppling of the Ba'athist regime represented the removal of the biggest stumbling block to an enduring settlement.

The regime fell with astonishing rapidity and Saddam Hussein was captured and subsequently executed. Though murderous unrest, numerous suicide bombings and the scourge of terrorism plagued many parts of Iraq during the subsequent occupation, Kurdistan remained an oasis of comparative tranquillity, increasing prosperity and religious tolerance. Deep political rivalries were set aside in the interest of the greater common good. This resulted in the consolidation of democracy in Kurdistan itself and also the appointment of Jalal Talabani as the president of Iraq – the first Kurdish leader to become the head of an internationally recognised state. Since 2003, the Kurdistan Region of Iraq has enjoyed unprecedented progress in terms of social and economic development, benefiting from a sense of stability and security rarely enjoyed in the past, as well as increased exposure to the advances and technology of the outside world.

One of the many tragedies in Kurdistan's recent history must surely be the death of Sami Abdul Rahman, who died with his elder son and more than 100 other Kurds when Islamist suicide bombers struck the headquarters of the two main Kurdish political parties in Erbil in February 2004. He was far more than his title of Deputy Leader of the KDP might suggest – a statesmanlike figure, British educated, who was an able diplomat for the Kurdish cause internationally and destined one day, many now agree, to lead his nation in the twenty-first century.

Sami Abdul Rahman Park celebrates his memory, and the monuments shown here (*opposite and left*) commemorate the tragic bombing and the names of those who died.

5

ECONOMY

Kurdistan's economy has been transformed in recent years. Since 2003 and the fall of Saddam Hussein stable and peaceful conditions have produced spectacular growth in all sectors. The country is now unrecognisable from the condition it was in 20 years ago, when prolonged re-development at the hands of Iraq had left it debilitated and in poverty.

Today, much of the economy depends upon the oil and gas sector, and, since 2009, Kurdistan has started to generate revenue from the export of its own oil. No doubt growth will continue in the future, as more investment pours in and workers come to the Region from other parts of the country.

Oil is the major source of the Region's recent prosperity, although, crucially, stability has provided the springboard for the further investment that is required in order to realise its potential.

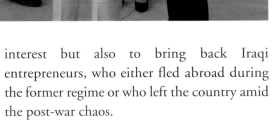

Alight at Erbil's new international airport, or book into one of its modern hotels, and you could find yourself rubbing shoulders with bankers from Jordan and Lebanon, construction magnates from Egypt and Turkey, or oilmen from Norway, Korea and the US.

After decades of physical and political isolation imposed at the hands of others, Iraq's Kurdistan Region has declared itself open for business.

Since the fall of the Ba'athist regime in April 2003, an impressive security record, combined with the emphasis by Kurdish authorities on creating a vibrant private sector, has lured a cosmopolitan array of visitors to sniff out business and investment opportunities in the rapidly diversifying economy.

Despite the near destruction of their social and economic base, a position in the toughest of regional neighbourhoods and the chronic security situation elsewhere in Iraq, the people of Kurdistan are busy carving out what they hope will be one of the most business-friendly environments in the Middle East. It is a tough sell. The Kurds have variously described themselves as 'the other Iraq', or the 'Gateway to Iraq'. Both slogans featured in international media campaigns, not only to attract foreign interest but also to bring back Iraqi entrepreneurs, who either fled abroad during the former regime or who left the country amid the post-war chaos.

Unprecedented sums of money have poured in after April 2003, a result in part of a deal struck with the federal government in Baghdad whereby the Kurdistan Regional Government gets 17 per cent of the national pie. While dependent on federal funds, the Kurds have sought to gain as much economic independence as possible.

The KRG and Baghdad have yet to agree, however, on a range of fundamental economic issues, including a national revenue-sharing law, and the management of Iraq's natural resources. These disputes, essentially political in nature, are unlikely to be resolved soon and may rumble on for some time.

Neverthless, spurred on by the nascent oil industry in Kurdistan, and a liberal investment law, there are now an estimated 105 private sector investment projects worth over US$16 billion in Erbil, Suleimaniah and Dohuk.

In October 2009, the Kurdistan Region hosted the fifth annual Erbil International Trade Fair, attracting some 750 companies from 29 different countries, the largest event so far.

Above:
The new terminal at Erbil airport is emblematic of Kurdistan's spectacular economic growth in the last few years. Erbil's new International Airport is designed to handle over 3 million passengers and 35,000 metric tonnes of cargo per year. Low air density at higher altitudes, and ground temperatures as high as 50°C in summer, mean that runways have had to be exceptionally long to meet the latest safety standards — the new 4.8km runway is the fifth longest public runway in the world and capable of handling the largest and heaviest aircraft, including the Boeing 747, the new double-decker Airbus A380 and the Antonov 225.

In his opening address, Nechirvan Barzani, the Prime Minister of the KRG, highlighted the commitment to an open-door policy.

'We hope the participating companies see the Kurdistan Region as a point of entry from which to engage in the reconstruction process for all of Iraq,' he said. 'Our efforts aim to rehabilitate the Kurdistan Region and all of Iraq in all sectors, based on interaction with the international community.'

It all appears a stark contrast to the rest of the country where economic nationalism and an addiction to centralised rule, never mind the recurring political and criminal violence, have deterred many potential investors.

Determined to avoid being dragged down by events elsewhere in Iraq, Kurdish leaders had little option but to turn to the private sector to try to revive an economic landscape still bearing the scars of the former regime.

'The aim of the KRG's strategy is to develop Kurdistan's physical, natural and, above all, human resources, in order to develop the economy to the long-term benefit of the people,' says Zeki Fattah, economic advisor to the KRG Prime Minister. The KRG's approach, he says, is to be mainly a manager of the economy, by nurturing a new and more innovative private sector that will produce goods and services in competitive and sustainable sectors. 'Under the KRG's strategy, the government is a partner of the private sector, but does not necessarily have a heavy or direct hand.'

Heresh Muharram, the chairman of the KRG Board of Investment, says the strategy is to throw open the doors to private investors but 'to be realistic'. The KRG's investment law, passed in 2006, is designed to foster private-sector involvement across the economy. It is one of the most liberal pieces of business legislation in the Middle East, offering foreign investors incentives including customs relief, tax holidays and the right to repatriate profits. Apart from policing and security, there appear to be no areas that are off-limits.

Mr Muharram lists agriculture, natural resources, energy provision, communications, tourism, education, health, construction and housing. 'We knew we lacked the infrastructure, and the expertise to develop it, so we invited in the responsible private sector,' he says. In addition to oil and gas, large investment projects are underway in electricity generation and the production of cement. Tourism, too, is attracting funds.

Senior KRG officials often hold out the model of Dubai, which they see as a good example of the smart use of oil wealth to develop an economy.

Envisaging the KRG as a logistics hub for its neighbours, Syria, Iran and Turkey, there are also plans to create something akin to Dubai's Jebel Ali Free Zone.

Certainly, the physical evidence of a new enterprise culture abounds. Take a tour around the outskirts of one of Kurdistan's three main cities: Erbil, Suleimaniah or Dohuk. Lining a network of newly built roads, construction projects are in progress seemingly at every turn: upscale housing complexes, high-rise office blocks, warehouses, car showrooms and sports and entertainment centres. Signs of rising personal wealth and fast-changing consumer habits are also not hard to find.

At weekends, drivers in shiny new cars ferry family members to any one of the swanky new shopping malls that have arisen on the edges of major towns. There they might refresh themselves with locally bottled Pepsi or Coca-Cola as they peruse aisles heaving with prized foreign consumer goods.

On hot summer evenings, families head for one of the new municipal parks, many of them built symbolically on land that used to belong to Saddam's Iraqi army. Or they may simply take off for the cool of the mountains, perhaps hiring a cabin at one of a number of new resorts. To those who know the area only through the depredations of the former regime, such scenes of relative normality may come as a shock. Especially compared with the rest of the country, Kurdistan has been making strides on every front, it appears.

Above:
Projects like the Nishtiman Trade Centre in Erbil are important signs of Kurdistan's growing prosperity. The billion-dollar project will eventually boast three 25-storey office towers.

Opposite top:
New skyscrapers are among the building projects that are the physical manifestation of Kurdistan's economic development.

Opposite below:
Building work in cities across Kurdistan is transforming the landscape. Cranes and construction equipment are a common sight across the country.

True, the three northern governorates had been ruling themselves since 1991, in the wake of Iraq's disastrous invasion of Kuwait and their own failed uprising against Baghdad. But these were troubled, dysfunctional times.

And though the threat of imminent destruction was removed under the protection of the allied air umbrella and the establishment of the safe haven, it wasn't until the US invasion in 2003, the subsequent unification of the Kurdistan Regional Government and the ratification of a new, federal constitution for Iraq, that the path cleared for genuine economic progress.

Iraq's relatively stable macroeconomic performance since 2003 – the exchange rate of the Iraqi dinar, the Federal Bank interest rate, and the inflation rate – also provided a sound launching pad for the Region. To assess the potential for future economic development, however, it is worth considering the legacies of the past, which inform and sometimes hamper today's situation.

When Saddam Hussein withdrew the Iraqi government's administration from Erbil, Dohuk and Suleimaniah in 1991, the land-locked Kurds were left to fend for themselves.

Against all odds, the Kurds held elections and formed a government that nurtured a degree of economic self-sufficiency.

But under self-rule they suffered twice over: from the effects of international sanctions imposed on Iraq following the invasion of Kuwait, and the internal trade embargo slapped on the region by Baghdad.

In the 1990s there were no airports in Kurdistan; access to any part of the Region was controlled by Turkey, Iran, Syria or Baghdad.

The Kurds' position along millennia-old trading routes between east and west allowed

KURDISTAN

The Ibrahim al-Khalil border crossing between Iraq and Turkey is a busy passage for trade and commerce between the two countries. The Turkish mountains loom large in the background. Trade across the border was crucial to keeping the Region alive during the 1990s.

Opposite and left:
Water is a commodity not to be taken for granted anywhere in the Middle East, but Kurdistan is blessed with numerous rivers carrying fresh mountain water down to the plains. Here we see a water filtration plant in the valley beneath Rowanduz, part of a network that ensures Kurdistan's self-sufficiency in water supplies.

for informal cross-border commerce (some call it 'smuggling') and the importation of goods from neighbouring Turkey and Iran, along with revenues from customs tariffs. The relative political stability provided breathing space for traders and small-scale businesses in cities and enabled towns to prosper.

Meanwhile, tanker trucks crossed daily from Turkey to fill up with Iraqi diesel fuel destined for the Turkish market. At least some of the money from the attendant border tolls went into the coffers of the Kurdish authority.

Such 'unofficial' trade provided a vital cash lifeline – several hundred million dollars per year, by some accounts – but also sowed the seeds for a ruinous dispute in the mid 1990s between the two main Kurdish parties (the KDP and PUK) over how the spoils should be divided.

As a result of that intercommunal bloodshed, in the late 90s the region split into two separate administrations, the KDP ruling Dohuk and Erbil, the PUK ruling Suleimaniah. Movement of people, services and goods between the two parts was severely restricted.

The Region got by, however. The rival administrations competed with each other to provide services for their citizens. The UN's oil-for-food programme ensured a safety net for poor families, and a start was made on the rebuilding of the infrastructure. International NGOs flooded into the region to execute contracts under Resolution 986.

But fighting for a share of the UN's crooked and mismanaged oil-for-food programme had a number of negative outcomes for Kurdistan's economy.

Perhaps the most lasting of these was the creation of a dependency culture. For example, the centralised purchasing of food and the import of foodstuffs from outside Iraq removed the incentive for Kurdish farmers to plant crops. The population became dependent on food rations.

The UN's desire to avoid upsetting Saddam by officially recognising the KRG meant that all oil-for-food projects had to pass first through Baghdad.

Large infrastructure projects were either delayed or canceled.

For all these reasons and more, it would be difficult to think of a greater leap in the Middle East than that made by the Kurds in the years following Saddam's removal.

in Lebanon, and twice as high as that recorded in Egypt and Jordan.

Building an economy almost from scratch is a huge task, however. Some have called the current era, not always positively, the Kurdish goldrush.

Zeki Fattah estimates that income per head in the Region amounted to US$6,000 per head in 2008, compared to US$5,000 the previous year, a rise of 20 per cent.

Contrast that with the situation prior to 2003, when, under self-rule, it was an estimated US$1500 per head. In real terms, says Mr Fattah, the new level of GDP per head is higher than the level recorded for Turkey, equal to that

It is clear that raw entrepreneurialism alone is not enough.

Mr Muharram of the Board of Investment concedes that authorities and regulators have struggled to keep pace with the new, fast-moving business environment. Without a coherent economic blueprint, development, particularly of the infrastructure, has often been adhoc and patchy in its implementation.

The economic upturn brought with it inflationary pressures, particularly in the property sector.

The intermittent arrival of large sums of budgetary cash from the federal government in Baghdad caused sudden fluctuations in the money supply and Kurdistan's nascent financial and planning institutions have been found wanting.

Kurdistan's economy has been held back by the lack of an effective modern banking sector connected to global financial institutions. Across all sectors of economic life, cash is still king.

Meanwhile, mismanagement and corruption, the ugly sisters of emerging economies everywhere, have also prevented the Kurdish Cinderella from going to the ball.

Another potentially negative side effect of the sudden influx of money from federal Iraqi coffers and rising foreign investment is that the gap between rich and poor in Kurdistan is becoming a chasm. Inflation has hit low-earners hard. Kurdistan is thus a study of contrasts. In city centres, warrens of down-at-heel shops and stalls nestle amid shiny glass-fronted buildings. Alongside new upscale housing developments in the suburbs, the residents of Saddam-era housing projects struggle in conditions more akin to shanty towns, with a lack of sewerage and other basic services. Electricity, though much improved across Kurdistan, is still erratic in poorer areas, the air blighted by the diesel fumes spewing out from ageing generators on every block. Ambitious but ill-planned construction projects lie half-built, abandoned.

Rural areas continue to empty, the result of a lack of jobs and investment.

The standard of primary health care and the broader provision of health in Kurdistan is a source of concern.

The education system and the provision of human resources are in need of a major overhaul if Kurdistan is to meet the needs of a modern market economy.

Moreover, the Region is still in effect a welfare state, the legacy of decades of Ba'ath party socialist planning and the Kurds' troubled history. Employment is dominated by a bloated government sector, which employs around 1.5 million people (in a region of 4 million or so inhabitants), many of them unproductive. Jobs in the civil service are largely given on the basis of party affiliation rather than merit.

Above:
With prosperity have come large scale shopping centres and supermarkets bringing a whole new way of life to the families of Erbil.

Opposite:
The 2006 International Trade Fair in Erbil attracted more than 800 Iraqi, Arab and international companies. It marked the emergence of Kurdistan as an important new market for consumer goods. Here trade delegates from US automobile companies exhibit the latest car models.

Right:
Former Prime Minister Nechirvan Barzani attends a trade fair and considers new imports with businessmen working to assist in developing technology in Kurdistan's agricultural sector.

Government officials acknowledge that the use of precious public funds as a substitute for unemployment is not sustainable in the long term.

With no manufacturing industry to speak of and a largely moribund agricultural sector, the Kurdistan Region is still heavily dependent on imports. In 2007, for example, some 65 per cent of its food was imported. This in a region once renowned for its agricultural produce.

Compounding the problems are a lack of information and a lack of transparency. Reliable social and economic data on which both government and business can take strategic decisions and allocate resources are scarce.

Although relatively free, the Region's media is dominated by political parties, another spillover from the days of resistance. Journalists today lack information about and knowledge of economic issues, and are thus unable to hold business and government to account in their reporting.

The 'independent' media outlets that do exist are desperately short of resources and training. The broader economy has not developed to the point where advertising revenues can sustain them.

The challenges to growth, then, are many and complex, as KRG leaders are the first to recognise. Their own performance – especially on the lack of transparency and the failure to tackle corruption – was severely judged by the electorate in the regional elections in July 2009.

Nevertheless, most international observers agree that as long as the KRG gets its policies and priorities right (it has made laudable progress in this regard but still lacks institutional maturity), and works hard to solve the hoary old problem of implementation and management (much work to be done here), then the economic outlook for the Kurdistan Region is bright.

The twin pillars of future economic growth for Kurdistan are generally regarded as the extractive industries and agriculture, both of which we shall now consider in more detail.

Oil and Natural Resources

'The large revenue that Iraq gets from the oil-fields might be used to help us instead of being spent on waging wars in these mountains and making the Kurds bitter and hostile. Remember the oil fields are in Kurdistan, so we have some right to ask for benefits from the revenue they earn. Yet all we seem to derive from our oil are bullets and bombs.'

Thus said Ismael Beg, the governor of Rowanduz, during a conversation with the New Zealand-born engineer A. M. Hamilton. But Ismael Beg's sentiments and remarkably prophetic thoughts about the Kurds and oil are still relevant today.

Anyone trying to unravel the complexities of the oil industry in post-Saddam Iraq would do well to consider this historical context.

Ever since oil was discovered in the huge Kirkuk oilfields in 1927, the Kurds have been marginalised as successive governments in Baghdad systematically excluded them from either the production of oil or its proceeds. It was no coincidence that the waves of Stalinesque 'Arabisation' campaigns conducted by the Ba'ath party, which resulted in the forced displacement of Kurds (as well as Turkmen and Christian minorities) from their villages and towns across northern Iraq, were at their most ruthless around the oilfields of Kirkuk.

It helps to explain why Kurds often mutter that the black gold beneath their feet has been more of a curse than a blessing.

It also provides the backdrop as to why since the removal of the Ba'athist regime in 2003, the Kurdistan Regional Government has fought doggedly with federal authorities in Baghdad – and in the face of significant pressure from US diplomats in Iraq to back down – to develop an oil industry of its own. It is not just about economics and the distribution of wealth.

The dispute over who controls and manages the natural resources in Kurdistan goes right to the very heart of Iraq's chances of survival as a democratic, federal state. In late 2005, after much haggling, Iraq's Kurds, Shias and Sunnis

Opposite:
The Taq Taq oilfield is one of the key new centres of Kurdistan's oil industry. Oil is pumped through the country's northern pipeline towards Turkey.

Below:
Former Prime Minister Nechirvan Barzani opens the valves of the Khurmala Dome plant in July 2009. The oil is sent to a refinery in Erbil and is converted into electricity, helping to meet the power needs of the Region.

agreed to clauses in Iraq's historic permanent constitution that essentially gave the federal government co-decision making powers over 'current' oilfields and left new and undeveloped fields to the producing governorates, or in the case of Kurdistan, the regions.

In order to allay suspicions in some quarters that Kurds were intent on using oil to lay the economic foundations for independence, the KRG accepted the principles behind Article 111 of the constitution, which provides that Iraq's oil and gas are owned by all of the people of Iraq in all of its regions and governorates. The KRG also announced that the proceeds from oil exports from the fields under their control would go automatically to the national pot. Which is when a national revenue-sharing agreement, if there were one, would kick in – and the Kurds would get their 17 per cent.

For the Kurds then, it was a test case for honouring constitutional agreements on regional autonomy, one that many believed the federal authorities failed.

Their ambitions were frustrated by political infighting with the Arabs in Baghdad who have long resisted the Kurdistan Region's wish to run its own oil industry.

The federal government held that contracts signed without its approval should be declared void. It refused to recognise the validity of contracts signed by the KRG, and said any company doing business with the Kurds would be blacklisted from oil projects in the rest of Iraq. Kurdish officials angrily denounced their approach as 'mischief-making'. The Kurds said they would never return to the days when Baghdad governments used oil revenues to buy tanks and helicopters to destroy their villages.

'Oil can either be a reason for Iraq breaking up, or the glue that binds it together,' says Ashti Hawrami, the KRG's Minister for Natural Resources, who has been instrumental in building the nascent Kurdish oil industry.

The appointment of Mr Hawrami – a seasoned oilman – in 2006 was a clear signal from the Kurdish authorities that they saw the region's oil and gas reserves – both potential and proven – as the primary spur not just of economic growth, but also of the internationalisation of Kurdistan's economy.

According to a USAID-funded report on the KRG's economic prospects, oil and gas production could provide between 5,000 and 6,000 jobs; support services alone could add another 11,000 to 13,000 people with employment. 'A variety of oilfield services, equipment and personnel will be needed to support extractive-industries sector-companies as they seek, find and produce crude oil, natural gas and mineral deposits,' the authors stated. All companies that signed contracts with the KRG had to pledge to a social

Below:
The Taq Taq energy plant is jointly run by Turkish Genel Enerji and Canadian ADDAX Petroleum company. The workforce running the refinery is also multinational.

Right:
Map of the oil infrastructure of Iraq.

offset programme, whether that be building kindergartens or funding Kurdish scholars through university.

There are political benefits, too. The prominent role played by Turkish companies in developing the fledgling oil industry in the Kurdistan Region of Iraq has already helped to reduce cross-border tensions.

The attractions of the Kurdistan Region of Iraq to prospective oil companies are not hard to see.

According to George Yacu, a US-trained geophysicist, who worked for the Iraqi National Oil Company from its inception, about 43.7 billion barrels (about 38 per cent) of Iraq's proven reserves of 115 billion barrels lie in the Kurdistan Region – including fields in Kirkuk and the disputed territories. Contrary to the conventional wisdom, says Mr Yacu, 'the

majority of these reserves lie within the governorate of Erbil, and not within Kirkuk.' He estimates that about 30 per cent of Iraq's potential reserves lie underneath the Kurdistan Region.

Adding to the bright prospects for the energy sector in the north is the presence of more than 200 trillion cubic feet of gas.

Aside from the disputes over control, management and revenues of Iraq's oil, the policy of the federal oil ministry in Baghdad has focused almost entirely on rehabilitating the existing fields in Iraq, damaged by years of wars and sanctions. The development of new fields was therefore put on the back burner. For the under-explored Kurdistan region, this was bad news.

'We had no alternative but to push ahead,' says Khaled Salih, a senior advisor to the KRG

Prime Minister and the Minister for Natural Resources. 'If we'd left it up to Baghdad, there would still be no oil industry in Kurdistan to this day.'

Despite the potential pitfalls, not least of which was their own inexperience with oil and gas, the KRG pressed on.

Beginning in 2002, Kurdish authorities began to sign exploration and production contracts with a number of independent and mid-sized foreign companies.

An important milestone occurred in 2007 when, in the absence of an Iraq-wide hydrocarbons law, the Kurdistan regional parliament debated and passed its own oil and gas law. The law was designed to comply in both letter and spirit with Iraq's federal constitution. The KRG also published a Model Contract based on international best practice.

Left:
The revived Kurdish energy sector has attracted investment from many multinational companies. The 1 June ceremony to celebrate the resumption of oil exports from Kurdistan was attended by executives from Turkey's Genel Enerji and Calgary-based ADDAX Petroleum.

Opposite below:
The ceremony was an occasion for celebration for Kurdish leaders and their people. Iraqi President Jalal Talabani and Kurdish Regional President Masoud Barzani opened the valve in a joyful moment that marked a major step forward in economic relations between Kurdistan and Turkey.

Then, in late 2007 the KRG published more than fifty exploration blocks and invited bids.

The KRG's approach revolved around production-sharing agreements, with the risk borne by the contractor/investor who gets a net profit share ranging from 9 to 12 per cent, depending on the exploration risks of the project.

In a first for Iraq, the state was reduced to a largely regulatory role.

The speed of the exploration and development subsequently took oil experts by surprise. To date, more than 35 investors from 15 countries have entered into some 30 contracts with the KRG.

Another milestone occurred on 1 June, 2009 when Mr Hawrami oversaw the launch of Kurdish oil exports through Iraq's northern pipeline to Turkey. On stage at a glitzy ceremony in Erbil, KRG President Masoud Barzani and Iraqi President Jalal Talabani together opened a symbolic valve allowing crude to flow from the first newly developed oilfields to come online for some thirty years.

The export-ready oil came from two fields: one at Tawke on the Turkish border, which was explored and developed by DNO, a Norwegian outfit. The other was at Taq Taq, (near Koi Sanjaq) the product of a joint venture between ADDAX, an independent exploration and development company quoted on the London and Toronto stock exchanges, and Genel Enerji of Turkey.

The Tawke field initially pumped 60,000 bpd. A newly constructed pipeline carried the crude from the production site, east of Zakho, to join the main northern pipeline on the Iraqi side of the Turkish border. Meanwhile, 40,000 bpd were trucked from the Taq Taq site to an export facility at Khurmala, where it was uploaded into the pipeline. A feeder pipeline to replace the tankers is on its way.

As other fields in the KRG are discovered and developed, the target is to produce 450,000 bpd by 2011, reaching one million bpd by the end of 2012.

In the summer of 2009, former KRG Prime Minister, Nechirvan Barzani, opened the largest private-sector refinery in Iraq, in Erbil governorate, able to process 75,000 bpd. Mr Barzani said the refinery would be able to generate vital products that would reduce dependence on foreign commodities, provide fuel for all vehicles and households for the Kurdistan Region. More refineries are expected to come online in the next two years.

Progress is also being made in exploiting the region's apparent abundance of natural gas. Gas from fields at Khor Mor and Chamchemal will be used primarily to fuel two power-generation plants outside Erbil and Suleimaniah. However, in the future, excess gas may well be exported, possibly to the Nabucco project in Turkey. Mr Hawrami says his ministry is also looking at the possibility of establishing a 'gas city' to create a centre for a downstream gas industry.

The Ministry of Natural Resources is meanwhile drafting a law to regulate mining activity in the Region. Despite a lack of reliable geological surveys, experts predict that the chief interest lies in a belt approximately 15–25 km wide that runs along Kurdistan's border with Iran and Turkey. The area is considered to offer 'high potential' for mineral deposits such as iron, chrome, nickel, platinum, gold, copper, barite and zinc.

With the commencement of crude exports, it appeared that relations between the KRG and Baghdad were at last on an upward turn. Iraq's export pipelines are controlled by the federal oil ministry, which agreed to allow the 'Kurdish' crude to flow.

The estimated $5 million a day (based on a price of US$50 per barrel) from the exports was helping to plug gaping holes that had appeared in Iraq's national coffers following the drop in international oil prices and the global economic crisis.

But the federal oil minister Hussein Sharastani soon threw a spanner into the works, saying that Baghdad would happily take the revenues but was under no obligation to pay the companies for their work. That was the KRG's problem, he said.

Neither was there progress on a new national hydrocarbons law nor on revenue-sharing. The two pieces of legislation are deemed to be vital to Iraq's future stability, but have been set aside for the time being.

Despite the challenges, the KRG is making impressive progress in establishing an oil industry within its region. Major discoveries have been made, and more are expected soon. New pipelines are being planned. Some have wryly suggested that Kurdistan should be renamed 'Krudistan'.

Agriculture

Agriculture is the historic backbone of Kurdistan's economy. For hundreds if not thousands of years, Kurdistan's lush mountain valleys and fertile rolling plains have been both the fruit basket and granary of Iraq, supplying the region, and beyond.

Accounts of Western travellers to the area in the early part of the last century note in some wonder the abundance and variety of produce they encountered – from the gallnuts that were collected each summer from the scrub oaks of Kurdistan for use in the tanneries of Baghdad, to the liquorice which grew alongside Kurdistan's rivers and was exported to Europe and the US.

Other exports from the Region consisted of wheat, barley, rice and various grains, gums, cheese, honey, raisins and other dried fruits. Locals, meanwhile, could feast themselves on the finest grapes – which grew on terraces that did not need irrigation – as well as pomegranates, walnuts, almonds, apples and apricots. Kurdistan's rivers also produced fish whose quality was appreciated for miles around.

Today, travel into the mountains or plains and you will no doubt come across the same rich assortment of quality produce. But you will also learn that its role in sustaining the local population and earning valuable revenue for rural communities is now much diminished.

Rural populations across the globe are gradually urbanising, a trend which has also touched Kurdistan. But here, farming was virtually – and deliberately – destroyed by the time the Kurds achieved self-rule in 1991.

During his genocidal Anfal (Spoils) Campaign against the Kurds in the late 1980s, Saddam's forces razed more than 4,000 villages and killed tens of thousands of civilians. Large parts of the rural population were forcibly evicted and resettled in specially constructed 'victory' towns, where the Ba'ath party security apparatus could keep a watchful eye.

Most of the villages have since been reconstructed, but the damage inflicted on a historic way of life has not.

According to Kurdish officials, the percentage of Kurds in agriculture has dropped from some 60 per cent to around 10 per cent in the past generation. As rural communities have

disappeared so too has generations of farming know-how, not to mention knowledge of rural crafts.

It was not just the brutality of the Ba'ath that was to blame. The UN's well-intentioned but ultimately misconceived oil-for-food programme introduced in the mid 90s proffered what appeared to be the final nail in the coffin of Kurdish agriculture. The centralised purchase of basic foodstuffs left Kurdish farmers with no viable market for their produce. Wheat, which Kurdistan has in abundance, was imported from as far away as Canada and Australia, sometimes as the result of corruption.

Today, according to USAID, over 80 per cent of the region's basic staples are imported.

An open border has created a market for often substandard or imported goods from Turkey, Iran or Syria.

An agricultural renaissance, then, is urgently needed. The political will of the KRG to restore Kurdish agriculture to its former glory days is evident; it is a central plank of its overall market-oriented development strategy. The authorities want to breathe new life back into rural Kurdistan. It would help to diversify the economy away from over-reliance on oil and gas. The modernisation of the agriculture sector would also be far less controversial than the extractive industries. The federal government in Baghdad is eager to ensure sustainable food supplies for the rest of Iraq.

The raw materials are certainly all there. Food is being grown and sold again. Kurdistan's share of Iraq's agricultural production is significant. It produces 50 per cent of the nation's wheat, 40 per cent of its barley, 98 per cent of its tobacco, 30 per cent of its cotton, and 50 per cent of its fruit.

The KRG designated 2009 as the year of agriculture. Industries such as poultry, grains, fruits and vegetables, and livestock were held up as opportunities for investment. Officials also think biotechnology could be a key factor in the Region's agricultural future.

Dr Anwar Abdullah, senior agricultural advisor to the KRG, says 'Investors are encouraged to make the best use of our flexible

Opposite:
Agriculture still has the power to contribute a significant part of Kurdistan's economy. Here, farmers gather hay just outside Erbil.

Below:
Many farmers still use traditional tools and equipment in their work. However, technological advances will be an important part of developing Kurdistan's farming sector in the future.

Investment Law, and will be most welcome in one of the last gardens of the Middle East.'

The most important 'export' market for the Kurdistan Region's agricultural production is the remainder of Iraq.

But as yet there is no overarching system of quality control for the region's produce, which is vital if Kurdistan is to become self-sufficient in food or export its produce overseas.

Moreover, according to USAID, until now Kurdistan's lack of reliable electricity, refrigerated storage, sorting, grading and packaging, transportation and knowledge of marketing has limited the marketing and sales options available to producers.

There is also a shortage of quality feed for livestock in the Kurdistan Region, due largely to overgrazing of rangelands and the lack of proper conservation crops and techniques by farmers.

Kurdistan's long years of isolation have left a farming sector that sorely needs to update itself with technological and educational advances.

In October 2009, produce from the Kurdistan Region was exhibited for the first time at the World International Food Fair in London. Given the right institutional support, packaging and marketing, it may not be long before it appears on European food tables too.

KURDISTAN TODAY

S ince it gained autonomy in 2004, Kurdistan has made spectacular strides forward in all areas. The most remarkable achievement has been a high level of security and stability; not a single coalition soldier has been killed in the region in the wake of the fall of Saddam Hussein in 2003. This has laid the foundation for sustained development: the economy has grown massively, a more accountable and effective political system has developed, and across society there is a renewed spirit of enterprise towards improving the condition of the country.

Few who sanctioned the construction of the Kurdish Parliament buildings in the time of Saddam Hussein would have foreseen the genuine and successful implementation of Kurdish democracy that they have come to house.

The southern parts of the geographic region known as Kurdistan were included in the modern Iraqi state at its founding in the 1920s. For most of the time since then, Kurds have been chafing at, or openly rebelling against, central rule in Baghdad.

The Kurdish movement in Iraq has rarely, if ever, pushed for full independence, at least not openly. It is true that many Kurds continue to say that self-determination is a 'natural' right. But they are ultimately a pragmatic people who are keenly aware of their geopolitical surroundings. Kurds have therefore tended to concentrate on gaining as much autonomy as possible from a succession of reluctant, often hostile, Arab-led regimes in Baghdad.

Before 1991, there were a number of still-born attempts at a negotiated settlement to solve the Kurdish issue in Iraq.

It was not until the aftermath of Saddam's disastrous invasion of Kuwait, and the creation by the Coalition Powers of a "safe haven," located north of the 36th parallel in Iraq, a line just south of Erbil, that self-rule became a reality, albeit a harsh one.

In May 1992, Kurdistan held its own elections, and in June of that year, the Kurdistan National Assembly began its sessions in Erbil. Thus, a Kurdish-led government was born, administering a territory roughly the size of Switzerland and covering the three northern governorates of Erbil, Dohuk and Suleimaniah.

This page:
The Kurdistan Parliament has 111 seats. Of these, eleven seats are specifically allocated to represent the Turkmen, Chaldean Assyrian Syriac, Armenian and minority communities in the country. There is also a legal requirement that 30 per cent of the representatives must be women.

Opposite:
Jalal Talabani and Masoud Barzani were once rival leaders of the PUK and KDP respectively. However, they have since set aside their differences, united in working towards the common goal of a better, more prosperous Kurdistan. They are the two most significant political figures in contemporary Kurdistan.

Despite myriad economic and social problems, domestic and international isolation, and a damaging conflict between the two main political factions in the mid 90s, the 13 years of self-rule before the US invasion of Iraq in 2003 provided the foundation for the ostensibly solid institutional structures that we see today.

These two rival political parties, the Kurdistan Democratic Party and the Patriotic Union of Kurdistan, have dominated local politics in recent decades. The two parties shared the government in Kurdistan until the mid 90s, when disputes over power, territory and money sparked a four-year period of conflict during which several hundred Kurds were killed.

Following a Washington-brokered ceasefire in 1998, the KDP and the PUK established separate KRG administrations, the KDP ruling Dohuk and Erbil, the PUK holding sway in Suleimaniah.

A Unified Kurdistan Regional Government

It was not until January 2006, however, that the parties announced a Unification Agreement to merge their administrations into one, unified Kurdistan Regional Government – KRG. Under the terms of this deal, representatives of each party would be assigned a balanced number of cabinet posts, with positions such as the speaker of parliament and the prime minister to be rotated between the two political parties. The two parties also negotiated a long-term election pact, which would see them campaign on joint tickets for regional and national elections.

The move came on the heels of an important milestone, when, in late 2005, a new and permanent constitution for Iraq enshrined federalism and parliamentary democracy as the post-dictatorship order.

Nechirvan Barzani became the first Prime Minister of the unified cabinet, while Adnan Mufti was named the speaker of parliament. The cabinet was faced with a number of

significant challenges, not the least of which included the formation of a government from parties which had recently been diametrically opposed. Nevertheless, during the period from 2006–2010, the KRG spearheaded unprecedented progress and growth throughout the Region, particularly in the spheres of economic activity, infrastructure, service, delivery and a modern framework for social development.

The cabinet began its work with the platform of delivering recognisable progress to the lives of citizens; among other things, this would be the best way to overcome the divide between political parties and unify all actors under the umbrella of creating a better Kurdistan Region. Improvements to roads, electricity delivery and water resource management have been of great importance. Efforts to rejuvenate the agriculture industry are vital to the well-being of many citizens, and therefore were prioritised.

At the same time, the Prime Minister and his cabinet acknowledged that the government could not and should not achieve these goals alone. Great emphasis was, therefore, placed on

the participation of the private sector as the driving force for economic and commercial development. The government was willing to act as a catalyst to stimulate investment, specifically foreign direct investment, through forming a viable government and a Region with an infrastructure and basic service delivery. However, it was understood that progress would depend heavily on private sector activity, and the Region embarked upon an appropriate framework to this end.

Two other strategic considerations were at the forefront of KRG policy: security and natural resource management. Nechirvan Barzani knew that insecurity was irreconcilable with the modernisation and progress of a new Kurdistan Region. An improved security architecture allowed the Region to move forward in a manner impossible elsewhere in Iraq.

Meanwhile, with stability, security and an investment-friendly economy, the KRG promoted cooperation with international oil companies to explore and develop oilfields. Coordination with the federal oil ministry was a major challenge, and the utilisation of the production-sharing agreement format was not

warmly received in Baghdad. Nevertheless, the KRG managed to attract some twenty five international oil companies, and in 2009 the Kurdistan Region pumped crude oil from two oilfields to the international market for the first time.

The KRG also undertook a complete revamping of its social programme, discussed in more detail below. The formation of the Judicial Council, as the third branch of government, was the landmark achievement in a number of initiatives designed to better apply the rule of law. Serious attention was paid to the the empowerment of women and women's rights, particularly the eradication of violence against women. The tolerance of all religions and ethnicities, always a source of pride, was of great importance as the Region continued to host thousands of families seeking a safe haven in the Region after fleeing other parts of Iraq.

Of greatest geopolitical significance was the rapprochement with Turkey. The thousands of troops which Turkey had amassed on the border had been causing concern to the KRG, and over the years no love had been lost between Erbil and Ankara. A number of behind-the-scenes meetings and continued KRG effort succeeded in establishing a way forward that would be mutually beneficial. Following the historic visit of the Turkish Foreign Minister to Erbil in late

2009, Turkey established its official Consulate in Erbil in March 2010, ushering in a new era of cooperation in bilateral relations. President Barzani's official visit to Turkey three months later, which included meetings with the Turkish President, Prime Minister, and Foreign Minister, further solidified the burgeoning partnership.

The ability of the Kurdish parties to unite their efforts in the interest of the Region as a whole has been instrumental to their development. The contribution of the cabinet in this regard cannot be overstated, and the phase of transition has facilitated improvement in all sectors of government activity. Prime Minister Barzani summed up the work of the first unified government in his 2009 farewell address: "We have restored security and stability to our beloved Kurdistan and established the foundation of civil life."

The Kurdistan National Assembly (since renamed the Parliament of the Kurdistan Region), the Kurdistan Regional Government, and the Kurdistan Region itself were all specifically recognised in the Iraqi Constitution, as were all of the Region's laws and contracts made since 1992. The Constitution also entitled federal regions in Iraq (Kurdistan being the only such entity to date) to draw up their own constitutions, though these should not contradict the basic precepts of the federal one.

Kurds have also played a key role in the federal government in Baghdad. Senior figures such as Jalal Talabani, the Iraqi President, Hoshyar Zebari, the Iraqi Foreign Minister, and Barham Salih, now the KRG Prime Minister but formerly the Iraqi Deputy Prime Minister, ensured that Kurdish interests were never far from the national agenda. Despite political differences back home, in Baghdad the Kurdish bloc maintained a united stance on key Kurdish issues such as the right to develop and manage natural resources within their region, Kirkuk and the disputed territories, and the funding of Peshmerga forces from the sovereign budget as part of a national defence system.

Following the January 2005 elections to the federal parliament in Baghdad, the Kurdistan Alliance, which comprised the KDP, the PUK and two moderate Islamist parties, formed the second largest bloc behind the main Shia grouping.

The Kurds became an important part of the government of national unity, headed by Prime Minister Nuri al-Maliki. Kurdish security forces meanwhile, made a significant contribution to fighting terrorism in central and northern Iraq. They stayed out of the Shia–Sunni sectarian warfare in 2006 and 2007 and helped to secure parts of the Iraqi capital.

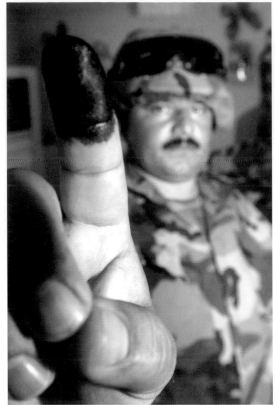

Kurdistan is, however, engaged in protracted disputes with the federal government in Baghdad over the precise borders within its territory and its right to control the economic resources within its territory. Although there have been violent incidents in the cities of Kirkuk and Mosul, which lie beyond the area currently administered by the KRG, the Kurdistan Region's territory itself has largely escaped the sectarian violence and terrorist warfare that has taken place in Iraq since the fall of the Ba'ath regime in 2003.

There have been suicide attacks in Erbil and Suleimaniah by Islamist extremists, but the Kurds have generally kept their region secure and stable. It is a matter of pride that not a single coalition soldier has been killed in the KRG-territory since 2003.

The Iraqi constitution granted the Kurdistan Region the right to provide its own internal security. This is accomplished through the work of the Peshmerga, the Asayish (security), Kurdish intelligence services and the police force. Together, these forces, which ultimately answer to Kurdistan Region President Masoud Barzani, have provided the most disciplined and loyal security apparatus seen in Iraq since the removal of Saddam.

There have been excesses, however. Rights groups such as Human Rights Watch and Amnesty International have raised concerns about actions taken by the Kurdish security forces. Arbitrary arrests and detentions without due process still occur, they say. Kurdish authorities accept that there have been problems and have publicly resolved to strengthen the overseeing of the security services. Like many administrations faced with an ever-present terrorist threat, striking the appropriate balance between security and liberty is an inevitable challenge.

One problem, and a source of much debate, is that the main political parties – the KDP and PUK – historically have employed rival armed forces and intelligence apparatus whose loyalty has been to the party first, rather than to the government.

The command structure of the two forces has now been unified, as has the KRG Ministry of Peshmerga Affairs, so that the 50,000 or so Peshmergas have become a part of the Kurdistan Region's official security structure – as regional guards – which is permitted under Iraq's constitution. The unification of the KRG Ministry of Interior was also a critical step forward in this regard.

Controversially, the two parties also still maintain separate intelligence structures. Commitments have been made to unify these agencies, but little progress has been achieved. One major stumbling block is the residual mutual distrust stemming from the parties' past rivalries.

Elections and Legislation

Since their historic first free elections in 1992, Kurds have embraced the democratic process with enthusiasm. There have been impressive voter turnouts for a succession of ballots to elect representatives of the three KRG governorates, the Kurdistan parliament, and the Iraqi Council of Representatives in Baghdad.

Elections for the Kurdistan Parliament must take place at least every four years. The last such vote was held on 25 July 2009. All citizens aged 18 or over and who are on the electoral register

The election held in July 2009 was a landmark occasion for the population of Kurdistan. People from all sectors of society turned out in numbers to demonstrate their commitment to the democratic process.

are eligible to vote in a direct, universal and secret ballot. To date, these polls have been organised on a system of proportional representation in which electors vote for a party's list of candidates, rather than for individual candidates, though the 2010 Iraqi national election did provide voters with the opportunity to vote for individuals.

Parties are allotted seats in proportion to the number of votes received; the success of candidates depends on their ranking on the party's slate. In the run-up to the July 2009 poll, the closed-list system was heavily criticised. This was the case largely because the rest of Iraq had ditched the party slate for an open-list system, which it was hoped would encourage better ties between representatives and their electorate.

The Kurdistan parliament comprises 111 seats. Of these, eleven seats are set aside for the minority communities that live within the

Left:
As an important figurehead for the country, the image of Masoud Barzani is widespread throughout the country. Although now he is a prominent statesman, many older members of the community will remember him as a freedom fighter for the Kurdish cause.

Opposite:
Barham Salih, prime minster of the Kurdistan Regional Government (third from left), chairs a meeting of his cabinet.

Region. Five seats go to Turkmen parties, five to Chaldean Assyrian Syriac representatives, and one to an Armenian.

The legal minimum quota of women MPs is set at 30 per cent of the legislature. In the current parliament, 39 of the 111 MPs are women. This is a higher percentage than in the Council of Representatives in Baghdad, where there is a 25 per cent quota for female MPs. There is, however, currently just one female cabinet member in the KRG out of a total of 19 ministers.

In accordance with provisions in the federal constitution of Iraq, the Kurdistan Parliament has broad powers to debate, legislate and scrutinise policies in a wide range of areas, including: health services, education and training, policing and security, natural resources, agriculture, housing, trade, industry and investment, social services and social affairs, transport and roads, culture and tourism, sport and leisure, ancient monuments and historic buildings. The Parliament shares legislative power with the federal authorities in the following areas (but priority is given to the Kurdistan Parliament's laws where there is a conflict): customs, power generation and its distribution, general planning and internal water resources. In addition, under Article 121 of the Iraqi federal constitution the Kurdistan Parliament has the right to amend the application of Iraq-wide legislation that falls outside the federal authorities' exclusive powers.

One of the Parliament's most important functions is to debate and ratify the KRG's annual budget. It also has powers to approve cabinet appointments and call ministers and their deputies to account for the performance of KRG ministries.

Until recently, the Kurdistan Parliament was largely passive in exercising the considerable powers at its disposal. Critics tended to dismiss it as a rubber stamp for the dominant political forces, the KDP and the PUK. Genuine debate was rare. But the institution is now slowly finding its feet, passing and scrutinising several important laws that provide a framework for the Region's social and economic advance. These include: an open investment law; a hydrocarbons (oil and gas) law for the Kurdistan Region; increased punishments for those committing so-called honour killings, which will be treated as murder; strict limits on the practice of polygamy; and a press law that guarantees freedom to speak and to publish. Moreover, the composition of the chamber following the July 2009 elections breathed new life into the Kurdistan legislature.

Parliament is still dominated by the KDP–PUK coalition. The speaker, Dr Kamal Kirkuki, is a member of the KDP; the deputy speaker, Dr Arslan Bayez, is a senior figure in the PUK. But the strong presence of a new group, the Goran (Change) list, led by the former PUK luminary Nawshirwan Mustafa, means that the traditional powers of the Kurdish political scene are unlikely to have things all their own way.

Out of 100 MPs elected (excluding the

eleven set aside for minorities): 59 belong to the Kurdistan List (KDP and PUK); Goran is represented by 25 MPs; 13 were elected on the Reform and Services List (including the Kurdistan Islamic Union, the Islamic Group in Kurdistan, the Kurdistan Socialist Democratic Party and the Toilers Party); the Islamic Movement List has two MPs; while one MP represents the Freedom and Social Justice List (Kurdistan Communist Party, Kurdistan Independent Work Party, Kurdistan Pro-Democratic Party, Democratic Movement of Kurdistan People).

The Goran list exploited a pronounced disaffection with the political status quo to mobilise significant numbers of young and middle-class voters, particularly in Suleimaniah province. The KDP/PUK bloc can still muster a comfortable majority, but they can no longer drive legislation through parliament with no opposition.

Indeed, the fledgling democratic state in Iraqi Kurdistan appears to have taken an important step away from what analysts have called a 'managed democracy' toward a more responsive political system characterised by genuine multiparty debate and deal-making.

The Executive

As well as electing a parliament in July 2009, the citizens of the Kurdistan Region voted simultaneously for the first time to directly elect a president, who leads the executive arm of government in the Kurdistan Region.

Masoud Barzani, the incumbent and head of the KDP, was returned with 69.8 per cent of the vote, making 1,266,392 ballots in his favour.

The President of the region charges the Prime Minister and the Deputy Prime Minister with forming a cabinet, under the terms of the Unification Agreement.

The Prime Minister then submits the names of his or her cabinet members to the parliament for confirmation. The Prime Minister heads the Council of Ministers (the cabinet) and is responsible for the day-to-day operation of the government.

He is responsible for the preparation of the Region's budget, and the design and implementation of KRG policies.

The current Prime Minister is Barham Salih, a senior member of the PUK and former Deputy Prime Minister of Iraq. His deputy is Azad Barwari, a leading figure in the KDP. Mr Salih leads a slimmed-down administration of 19 ministers.

Until he took office in October 2009, the KRG cabinet comprised an unwieldy 43 ministers. This was largely the legacy of the unification of the two administrations in 2006.

Prime Minister Salih has committed his cabinet to administrative and financial reform, vowing to implement anti-corruption measures initiated by the previous cabinet and ensure transparency. He also plans to reduce political party interference in governmental affairs by taking civil service appointments out of the hands of party and tribal leaders, and putting them into the hands of a civil service commission. One of the biggest challenges to the efficient working of the KRG is the weight of bureaucracy. Some 70 per cent of the KRG budget goes to pay for the state sector, where government jobs tend to be distributed largely along political or tribal lines. Given a shortage of jobs in the private sector and the absence of a welfare system in Kurdistan, getting onto the government's payroll is seen as an easy route to financial security by many families. Reforming the civil service and the state sector in general will need to be a priority for future governments.

Mr Salih said the KRG will build on the Kurdistan Region's considerable economic progress and improved living standards by further developing schools and higher education, health, agriculture, irrigation and roads, and by resolving the housing problems for low-income citizens, increasing the income level of the individual and the living standards of the lower class. 'The government will promote political freedom and public determination,' he said. 'We will encourage civil society and the media to play a greater and more constructive role in promoting public opinion and expanding the circle of democracy.' Mr Salih also emphasised the need to give young people and women 'the encouragement and space' to participate in the Kurdistan Region's economic, social and political affairs.

Social Welfare

There is no organised welfare system in Kurdistan, but the huge government sector — which employs an estimated 1.2 million people (some 80 per cent of the total workforce) — means the whole Region is in effect a welfare state. It is a huge drain on government coffers, reinforcing a dependency culture that was born amid the political and economic centralism of the former Ba'ath regime, and then flourished under the oil-for-food programme in the latter part of the 1990s. Nevertheless, being on the government payroll does act somehow as a

social safety net, and reforming the system will need to be handled carefully.

The needs of low-income families in Kurdistan in regard to shelter, clothes, food and fuel oil are met by a combination of contributions from non-government organisations, political parties, local mosques, tribal and familial relations, and government food rations.

The widows of men who were killed during the Anfal Campaign or in the struggle against the Ba'ath regime receive a pension and other help from the KRG Ministry of Martyrs and Anfal Affairs. The government has also engaged in a large low-cost housing programme, where purchasers are provided with 50 per cent of the cost of a new house.

The Health Sector

The health sector in Kurdistan is an area that has been targeted for urgent reform. Health experts perceive huge challenges for KRG authorities if they are to create a modern sustainable system that meets the health needs of the growing populace. Like most pillars of Kurdistan's public service provision, the health sector struggled to survive after Saddam withdrew the Iraqi administration from the area after 1991. Kurdistan found itself obliged, unlike the rest of Iraq, to build up a health hierarchy from almost nothing.

Sanctions and civil conflict in the 1990s that led to the temporary division of the region into two separate administrations made the job of unifying the healthcare system even more difficult. Since 2003, health officials in the Kurdistan Region complain that the health ministry in Baghdad has - either deliberately or through malpractice - withheld its rightful share of quality medicine and supplies.

The Region is still coping with the negative effects of chemical-weapon attacks on physical and mental health, including congenital diseases, the very high prevalence of an aggressive type of breast cancer and of congenital heart disease, and pollution of many

The picturesque graveyard of Sayyid Sadiq in the east of Kurdistan would house a number of war dead from the long years of conflict with Iran. Peacetime has brought growth and prosperity to the formerly troubled lives of these villagers.

water sources by arsenic. In addition, Kurdistan's health system has come under further strain from thousands of Iraqis who have sought sanctuary from the violence elsewhere in Iraq.

Healthcare in Kurdistan is not a structured hierarchy. It is expensive to maintain and resources are not always allocated as well as they could be, with the result that progress has not always been achieved as fast as targeted. There are many overlapping authorities; and as no clear line exists between public and private healthcare, the public system in effect subsidises the private one. Experts and health officials agree on the need to establish a realistic blueprint for knitting the whole system together.

In recent years, the Ministry of Health has been trying to change the focus of its strategy away from building large, specialised institutions and has confirmed that they would like to see these left largely to partnerships with the private sector. Instead, the emphasis will be on reforming the primary healthcare system. However, it is worth noting that, with some 466 primary health centres for a population of 3.5 million (according to the World Health Organization), the KRG is better provisioned than the rest of Iraq.

Such statistics can be deceptive. Ninety-five per cent of Kurds use the rudimentary primary healthcare system, but too many patients are being sent to hospitals when they could receive simple treatment, says former KRG Minister of Health Dr Ziryan Yones. The lack of a proper referral system means public hospitals are unnecessarily overcrowded – problems that can only be fixed by facilitating an increase in capacity and increasing funding generally.

Medical education will need to be another priority. Training staff in the health sector (some 6,000 doctors, including 600 specialists) on the latest scientific medical advances and the use of state-of-the-art medical technology will be critical.

The KRG's new investment law has encouraged health specialists to start their own private clinics, hospitals and pharmaceutical

plants. They have been supported with free land and other assistance in order to implement ministerial plans. The support of the public sector is being encouraged, through the private sector, to provide additional services.

The Media in Kurdistan

The Kurdistan Region enjoys a media scene which is today far livelier than under Saddam Hussein's rule, with an impressive array of newspapers, magazines, terrestrial and satellite TV stations, radio stations and websites. Kurdish leaders and lawmakers have committed the Region to freedom of speech and freedom

of the press. In 2008, the Kurdistan Parliament passed a revised media law that protects journalists' rights and decriminalises libel. Journalists are free to write, print and broadcast in any language.

The roots of these freedoms go back as far as the dark days of the Ba'ath regime, when Kurdish leaders encouraged foreign media into Kurdistan, and that same open-door policy remains in place today. Compared to the rest of Iraq and the region, visiting journalists continue to move around and report, safely and freely.

Despite the plethora of domestic media outlets, some of which are outspoken in their criticism of the political establishment, there always remains room for more objective news

coverage and genuine investigative reporting.

Part of that development will come hand in hand with economic growth. The private sector in Kurdistan has not yet developed to the extent that revenue from sales and advertising can fully fund professional media outlets as they do in the West. Kurdish media organisations rely instead on backing from their funders, most of which are political parties, individual politicians or the government. Their reports and analyses are tailored accordingly. This connection to a cause or to a prominent individual is partly a legacy from the days of resistance to Ba'ath party rule, when Kurdish journalists were forced to work underground and their work was seen as a vital part of the battle against dictatorship.

Journalists tend to be relatively poorly paid, with few training opportunities and relatively little scope for career development. Loyalty to party and the ability to air an opinion are more valued by media managers and editors than accurate reporting by their staff on the events and issues of the day. No commonly agreed standard of journalistic ethics yet exists.

Hiwa Osman, the Iraq Director of the Institute of War and Peace Reporting, and former media advisor to Iraqi President Jalal Talabani, says no single outlet is providing comprehensive coverage of most stories, which does not help citizens to understand the political situation. 'It is quite rare these days to find a news report that has both sides of the story,' he says. 'Instead they are split, with the independent media representing the opposition and the party media representing the government. For Kurdistan to develop a healthy media scene, there needs to be credible sources of news and information, and not just opinions.'

The Region is home to several, powerful 24-hour satellite television stations, to which, for want of an alternative, the public turns for regional news. (Most households have satellite receivers.)

The first to hit the airwaves, in 1999, was the KDP's Kurdistan Satellite TV based in Salah-al-Din, north of Erbil. Another KDP-owned

Zagros TV, one of a growing number of local broadcasting services, puts out entertainment and news over ten channels, largely in Karmanji dialect. There are six news broadcasts a day, with the 9 p.m. slot being the major live news round-up *(above left and right)*.

The humble newsvendor shown here *(opposite)* is a local hero, known for his bravery in manning his newsstand through more troubled times. It is unlikely he could ever have foreseen the range and depth of material his stall was to come to hold as standard.

channel, Zagros TV, broadcasts from Erbil. The PUK, meanwhile, operates KurdSat, based in Suleimaniah. More recently, the new opposition grouping, Goran (Change), established its TV channel, the Kurdistan News Network. The Kurdistan Islamic Union, the fourth largest of Kurdistan's political groups, also has its own television station. The channels mix entertainment with news that tends to be slanted towards their own political allegiance. In addition to the satellite channels, there are dozens of terrestrial TV stations, most of them run by political parties.

The PUK publishes two daily newspapers: *Kurdistani Nuwe*, and the Arabic-language *al-Ittihad*. PUK politicians also fund the *Aso* daily. The KDP publishes the Khabat and Arabic-language *al-Ta'akhi* dailies. Goran's founder, Nawshirwan Mustafa, also set up a daily newspaper, *Rozhnama*. Other important journals include opposition outlets such as *Hawlati* and *Awene*, which are published twice-

weekly, the PUK-funded *Chawder* and the Kurdistan Islamic Union's weekly *Yekgirtu*. None of these has massive circulations, though reliable data does not exist. *Hawlati* has one of the largest readerships, printing some 20,000 copies.

The Region's radio scene tends also to be divided along political parties. Radio Nawa, a 24-hour news station which launched across the Region in 2005, could be considered an exception, although its touted neutrality came under question during the July 2009 election campaign when its director campaigned for the Goran list.

The growth of blogging, social networking and Kurdish-related websites, many of them operated by members of the Kurdish diaspora in Europe, has brought fresh air to the party-dominated media landscape in Kurdistan. Though here again, journalistic standards are often poor, with contributors often passing off rumour and innuendo for real reporting.

The Justice System

In May 2009, KRG Prime Minister Nechirvan Barzani officially inaugurated the new Judicial Council headquarters in Erbil. The building was, said the Prime Minister, both a physical and symbolic expression of the KRG's commitment to an independent judiciary and respect for human rights and the rule of law.

'We in the KRG face many challenges ahead of us… no challenge is more important than strengthening the authority and independence of our judicial system,' said Mr Barzani in his opening address. 'Good governance goes hand in hand with the application of the rule of law,' he added.

It was a theme often repeated by the former premier during his term in office. But, until 2008, Kurdish authorities had largely failed to put flesh on the assortment of commitments and plans for a much-needed change in the legal landscape.

Strengthening the judiciary and setting it free was seen as a key part of the KRG's attempts to add steel to its institutional backbone. With the Region opening up to foreign investment and the government's stated commitment to transparency, democracy and human rights, the legal system was simply not fit for the purpose.

Unlike in the rest of Iraq, where the judiciary was independent following regime change in 2003, in Kurdistan it remained under the direct control of the KRG Ministry of Justice. The lack of reform was in part a legacy of the Region's troubled history. The Kurds had certainly done well under difficult circumstances to maintain a legal system following the withdrawal of the Ba'athists' administration in 1991. But the separate government structures set up by the KDP and the PUK in the aftermath of the internal conflict of the mid-90s resulted in two separate justice ministries and Courts of Cassation, one for the Erbil and Dohuk governorates and one for the Suleimaniah governorate. The domination of the KDP and PUK in their respective strongholds brought about complaints of political interference in the work

Above:
Kurdistan has a vibrant and growing media which is consumed avidly by its population. High literacy rates and improving levels of education are helping to produce an increasingly discerning and well-informed public.

Opposite:
Kurdistan's younger generation are keen to embrace Western-style trends and Kurdish society as a whole is rapidly changing to absorb new fashions and cultural mores.

Left:
The Ministry of Justice, in coordination with the Judicial Council, supports the principle of an independent judiciary established in 2009 – a vital step in Kurdish self-rule.

of the courts. 'Wasta', or favouritism, and tribal and religious influences on judges remained a concern. The near isolation of the Region also meant huge problems in training judges and other legal staff. There was, in addition, an almost total lack of transparency.

The unification of the KRG in July 2006 provided a solid platform for change. After a comprehensive review, with the involvement of international legal experts, a consensus emerged among authorities that the time for concrete action had come.

In 2008, the Kurdistan Region's judiciary was formally separated from the executive and legislative branches of government to create an independent body. The judiciary was separated from the Ministry of Justice, put under the authority of a new Judicial Council headed by the Chief Justice, and allocated its own budget to allow self-administration. Since then, the judiciary has been learning to stand on its own feet, be objective and uphold the rule of law. Now there is one Court of Cassation and one Ministry of Justice for the entire region, both based in Erbil.

The reforms will take time to bed down, but they are already delivering a larger role for the courts in enforcing individual rights and reviewing legislation and administrative acts.

The structure of the courts in Kurdistan is similar to that in the rest of Iraq. Residents of Kurdistan are obliged to bring claims arising in Kurdistan before the Kurdish courts.

The Kurdistan Court of Cassation is the highest court of appeal in Kurdistan. It is independent of the Court of Cassation in Baghdad, which has no powers to review the judgments of its Kurdish counterpart.

Similarly, the Federal Supreme Court in Iraq, when it is fully operational, does not have the authority to review or overturn Kurdish laws. It may only consider the constitutionality of national acts or laws.

Despite the discrete nature of the Kurdistan and federal judicial authorities in Iraq, there are ongoing efforts to increase cooperation and coordination between the two bodies. At the end of 2006, there were 156 judges in

Kurdistan, including 97 in the governorates of Erbil and Dohuk, and 59 in the governorate of Suleimaniah. Almost all the judges are men.

According to a study in late 2006 by the Iraq Legal Development Project, (under the auspices of the American Bar Association) there are hopes that the stable security situation, and a new political will to strengthen the legal system in Kurdistan 'will lead to a judiciary that is better resourced, more representative of the Kurdish society, and independent of external influences.'

Education

In the wake of the First Gulf war, in 1991, Saddam's regime withdrew its entire administration from the Kurdistan region. Already hit hard by the Anfal Campaign of the previous decade that devastated rural communities, crucial services such as education now faced the prospect of disintegration.

It was the dedication of Kurdistan's teachers, who decided to restart schools by themselves, many going without pay for six months, which

ensured a generation of Kurdish children did not completely miss out on formal education.

The challenge was huge, recalls Mohamed Abdullah, who was a primary school teacher at the time and who now works in Erbil's education directorate. 'The school buildings were empty and in a sorry state of repair,' he says. 'There were no tables, desks, blackboards, or chalk. But just as serious was that the few textbooks we had available were infected with Ba'athist ideology. Printing new revised textbooks would cost time and money, and anyway the printing presses in the Region could only provide a fraction of the schools' requirements.'

In the classroom, improvisation was thus the order of the day, with teaching staff often asking children to blank out, or simply ignore, texts that glorified Saddam's rule.

Meanwhile, the new self-ruled Kurdish authorities set about reconstructing schools in urban areas and in the thousands of villages that had been destroyed during the Anfal Campaign. Here, too, a certain inventiveness was required. Former regime intelligence headquarters, abandoned mosques and empty

factories were all deployed in the battle to provide a physical infrastructure in which children could safely learn.

The period from 1991 until 2003 was a fraught one for the Kurds. International isolation, internal sanctions on the Region from Baghdad and conflict between the KDP and the PUK that resulted in mass displacement of families and the establishment of two rival administrations made life extremely difficult for students and educators alike. Dr Mohammed Sadiq, a former president of Salahaddin University in Erbil, describes it as follows:

'We had no legitimate links to the outside world. We were cut off. Borders were closed. The research frontiers were also shut off, because of our lack of interaction and access. We did not even have links with Iraqi universities.' It was not until after the removal of the regime in April 2003, he says, that Kurdistan's education sector was at last able to reconnect to the world.

It is widely acknowledged in the Region that the legacy of those tough 13 years has led to multiple problems that will take time, perseverance and, of course, the right policy strategies to overcome.

Despite a large building programme, there remains a chronic shortage of classrooms in which to educate the Region's youth. Most schools have two shifts of students per day. They still lack equipment and good maintenance. Rates of illiteracy, especially in rural areas and among girls, remain unacceptably high.

The number of school-age children in Kurdistan has increased exponentially in recent years, putting further strain on resources. In the 2008–2009 academic year, 1,335,313 pupils attended school in the Kurdistan Region, 96 per cent of them in the primary and secondary systems.

The higher education sector, despite the addition of several new universities (including, since 2003, the independently run University of Kurdistan-Hawler and the American University in Suleimaniah), struggles to accommodate the increasing number of secondary school graduates. An estimated 76,000 students are in tertiary education at any one time, squeezing in to just seven institutions. The pressure to absorb ever-greater numbers sometimes clashes with the Kurds' stated aim of increasing quality of instruction across the board.

Experts also point to challenges ahead in terms of quality of teacher training and the reform of the curricula. Moreover, the education sector in the Region is still highly centralised, with a government bureaucracy that can place unnecessary burdens on initiative. Senior appointments are too often influenced by political considerations.

Nevertheless, in the last three years, a more coherent vision for a modern education system in the Kurdistan Region has been emerging.

In May 2007, at the KRG Ministry of Education in Erbil nearly five hundred education experts gathered for a major conference on the future of education in the region. It proved a launching-pad for a far-reaching reform programme that is now under way.

Dr Dilshad Abdulrahman Mohammed, the former KRG Minister of Education who introduced the reforms with the backing of the then Prime Minister Nechirvan Barzani, says that for the first time Kurdistan has a basic and secondary education system designed to meet the needs of 'a modern, democratic, pluralist and market-oriented society.'

The opportunity of access to a free and fair education system should be available to all without prejudice, he says. 'The goal is to prepare and educate the next generation to become good, responsible, well-rounded citizens with an understanding of local and global issues and ideas and the capacity to think and act for themselves.' The old system of learning by rote will be replaced by a new, interactive, student-centred approach.

Children are required by law to attend school full-time from the age of six and complete grades 1–9. Then, the secondary stage will take pupils from 10–12, preparing them either for further education or to compete in the job market. The secondary system comprises both academic and vocational schools (where students can study agriculture, industry or commerce).

Education is mostly in Kurdish. In places it is conducted in Assyrian or Turkmen to reflect the region's demographic diversity. Arabic will be taught as a second language. The new system also envisages the teaching of English from grade 1.

Private educational institutions in Kurdistan are flourishing, with many wealthier parents opting out of the state system. The most noteworthy of these is probably The International School of Choueifat, whose large campus – designed to house up to 2500 students – opened on the edge of Erbil in the summer of 2008.

Education ministry officials say they are relaxed about the growth of private education but that they will act to ensure the basic standards in accordance with the law. Many educators in Kurdistan believe that, anyway, government bureaucrats should be taking a more hands-off approach to education. Changing the centralising mindset will take time, however.

Meanwhile, in the tertiary sector, the KRG says it is committed to assisting its public universities and to facilitating its private universities.

There are currently seven universities in the Kurdistan Region, with the three largest being Salahaddin University in Erbil, the University of Suleimaniah, and the University of Dohuk. They offer studies in various subjects leading to specialised diplomas, bachelor and master degrees, and doctorates. Two new universities teach exclusively in English: the University of Kurdistan-Hawler, and the American University of Iraq - Suleimaniah, and Ishik University, in Erbil, also teaches in English across a wide range of disciplines.

Educational standards in universities are slowly improving but still have some way to go. Again, universities need to be freer from government interference. Aware of the problems, university authorities desire more independence and want to promote the internationalisation of their institutions – in teaching and research.

They aim to draw back the educated diaspora of Kurdistan, with attractive research and teaching positions in the natural sciences, management, law and the applied social sciences.

7 | LOOKING AHEAD

The future for Kurdistan looks bright. If the country continues the spectacular economic growth it has achieved since the fall of the Baathist regime, then it will enjoy great prosperity in the years to come. This prosperity will depend on the successful resolution of a number of issues, including final settlement over the precise borders of the Kurdish territories, the maintenance of good relations with neighbours, and the continued development of effective organs of state that can implement further reconstruction and economic development.

Exploitation of oil reserves and the increasing trade that comes from Kurdistan's position as a trusted hub for the region's commerce will both be at the core of the Kurdish economy for the future. Tourism will be a third pillar of that economy – the dramatic landscapes such as the one shown here are already a popular destination for Iraqi Arabs from the south and visitor numbers look set to increase, coming from an ever-wider catchment area via the central hub of Erbil's major new international airport.

At the end of 2009, the situation in Iraq was still in a great flux. The bloody civil war between armed Shia and Sunni groups had mostly subsided but, disturbingly, Islamist and Baathist militants remained capable of mounting devastating attacks on civilian and government targets outside the Kurdistan region.

With US combat forces set to withdraw, the ability of Iraq's fledgling forces to maintain security unaided remained open to question. So too did the ability of the country's political class to agree on how the country should be governed. Or indeed the willingness of the 'international community,' meaning principally the US, to exert the diplomatic effort required to foster what author and constitutional expert Brendon O' Leary has termed a withdrawal from Iraq 'with integrity.'

Since 2003, the Kurdistan Region had been Iraq's safest and most stable area. Its economy and its institutions are beginning to flourish. Yet the Kurds remained nervous.

Tensions between the KRG and Baghdad, between Kurds and Arabs in the 'disputed' territories abutting the current Kurdistan Region, and the unwelcome prospect of the pullout of the US military reveal apprehension and deep-seated fears of abandonment.

On the political front, several interlocking issues look set to dominate the next crucial period in terms of relations between the regional and federal authorities in Erbil and Baghdad, respectively.

First, and most important, is a decision on the actual boundaries of the Kurdistan Region (the final status of the disputed territories).

Below:
President Masoud Barzani has been careful to ensure comfortable relations with the Kurds' Arab neighbours. He is seen here on a state visit to see HRH King Abdullah of Saudi Arabia in Riyadh.

Agreement is needed on the much-delayed national revenue-sharing law, and a national hydrocarbons law to regulate oil and gas. The debate over the status of the Kurdish Peshmerga forces, and power-sharing mechanisms at the federal level also cried out for settlement.

The Kurds have insisted that the solutions to all these challenges lay in Iraq's permanent constitution, which was passed by a substantial majority of Iraqis in 2005. Kurdistan Region President Masoud Barzani called the constitution 'our potent weapon.'

However, many Arab politicians, especially from the Sunni side, have placed their hopes in a promised revision of the constitution to create a more centralized system of government.

Their strategy apparently, is to delay the issues that most affect them (eg Kirkuk and oil) until the Baghdad government is strong enough to impose a solution on the KRG authorities. This approach has angered and frustrated Kurds.

Such a strategy also seemed to overlook the reality that though reforms to the constitution were possible, the Kurds possess an effective veto on changes to the document, which they would likely use if proposed reforms meant diluting the federal nature of constitutional provisions.

After the national elections in 2010, whichever Arab-led bloc forms the next federal government will find it difficult to govern without the Kurds on board.

In any case, argues Brendan O'Leary, author of 'How to Get out of Iraq with Integrity' and a former advisor to the KRG, 'no representative democratic Arab politicians in Iraq, whatever their views on other questions, proposes the complete unwinding of the constitutional rights of the Kurdistan Region.'

Disputed Internal Boundaries

The most explosive political issue facing Iraq lay in the continued debate among Kurds and Arabs over the future status of Kirkuk and the disputed territories.

The areas in question run in a northwesterly arc from Mandali on the border with Iran to Sinjar, which abuts Iraq's border with Syria. They are at the heart of what General Ray Odierno, the commander of US forces in Iraq, termed 'the driving force' of instability in the country.

These areas traverse five governorates and are home to some 3 million people, about 11 percent of Iraq's population. Kurds are in the majority, but there are also significant populations of Arabs, Turkomen, Yezidis, Chaldeans, Assyrians, and other ethnic groups, each with their own anxieties and aspirations.

Residents of these territories remain mired in uncertainty, waiting more in hope than expectation for Iraq's post-Saddam political classes to find a solution to an issue that has beset the country since its creation in the 1920s.

Prior to 2003, the territories were subject to a systematic campaign of ethnic cleansing called 'Arabisation.' Large numbers of Kurds, along with Turkomen, Yezidi and Christians were forcibly uprooted from their towns, villages and cities, while Arab settlers were brought in from the south, receiving monetary awards from the government. Arabisation was particularly brutal around the city of Kirkuk and along the border areas with Iran and Syria. It left a poisonous legacy for Iraq's post-dictatorship era.

For Kurds, resolving the status of the disputed territories is a bellwether for their chances of long-term reconciliation with the Arab-led state of Iraq. Kurds argue that historically and geographically these areas are part of Kurdistan and should belong to their semiautonomous region. But they insist this should be done through a legal and democratic process. Specifically, they want to see the implementation of Article 140 of Iraq's constitution, which provides a framework for settling the issues. It culminates in a referendum over the future status of the disputed territories.

After the fall of Saddam Hussein's regime and the collapse of the Iraqi army in 2003, Kurdish peshmerga forces moved into areas south of the previously accepted KRG-administrated area to provide protection for the

Above:
Kurdish society is highly diverse and incorporating all the wishes and ambitions of its different communities will be crucial in the future. In the city of Erbil there are large numbers of Chaldean and Assyrian Christians as well as the majority Muslim population. Christmas, celebrated here with an inflated Santa Claus suspended by the mosque, is an important time for them to celebrate their identity and community.

Left:
US President Barack Obama invited President Barzani and his delegation to the White House in January 2010 to discuss developments in the Kurdistan Region and throughout Iraq.

population – which they largely did – with approval from the US-led Multi-National Force in Iraq. But it also gave them de facto control over land whose legal status had not yet been finalised.

Arab and Turkomen politicians in the disputed territories voiced loud opposition to Kurdish plans to alter Iraq's internal boundaries, drawn under the previous regime. They accused the KRG of sending large numbers of Kurds into the disputed areas in order to create facts on the ground ahead of any future vote on their status. They charged the peshmerga with using heavy-handed tactics in disputed areas under their control.

They also began to use the term 'Kurdification,' as though the process of allowing Kurds to return to their former lands was somehow the moral equivalent to Arabisation. To the consternation of the Kurds,

the term soon entered the vocabulary of some diplomats in Baghdad, who talked in typically patronizing tones of Kurdish 'overreach.'

Meanwhile, in Baghdad some Arab nationalist politicians saw their chance to gain capital from the KRG's moves. Anti-Kurdish rhetoric grew. In laying claim to Kirkuk and the disputed territories, some claimed, Kurds were trying to break up Iraq and establish an independent state.

An anti-KRG grouping led by Sunni Arabs gained control of Nineveh governorate (home to the volatile city of Mosul) in the provincial elections of 2009. The Nineveh leadership refused to relinquish senior provincial posts to pro-Kurdish groups. And as the federal Iraqi government grew in strength, so it began to nibble away at Kurdish influence in areas adjacent to the official KRG region.

Several tense standoffs ensued between Iraqi security forces and peshmerga along what has become known as the 'trigger line' marking the divide between Arabs and Kurds.

The uncertainty provided space for Islamist militant groups belonging to Al Qaeda to attempt to foment inter-communal violence. Beginning in 2007, a series of bombings targeting the minority Turkmen, Shabak, Yazidi and Christian communities in these areas saw all sides accuse each other of responsibility.

US commanders feared such incidents could escalate into full-blown conflict if allowed to fester.

They brokered talks between Kurdish commanders and the Baghdad government to set up joint patrols, including, vitally, a US presence, in the provinces of Diyala and Nineveh, the most violent areas in the north.

In the short-term at least, such joint patrols

Below:
The status of the city of Kirkuk is a critical issue that will need to be resolved in the years to come. It is an ethnically diverse city with large communities of Arabs, Kurds and Turkmens. On the left of the picture is a portrait of Ali Madan, a popular Kurdish singer and to the right is a statue of Atta Kharalla, a Turkmen leader executed in 1959.

look likely to help to reduce tensions. But there is also a danger that the presence of US troops would provide a disincentive to the various sides to find a political solution to their differences. Some observers suggested it could make them more reliant on the US at the same time as the US was planning to withdraw.

Kurdish leadership has requested greater US engagement in terms of diplomacy and political brokering to help identify a lasting solution to the disputed territories and thereby to Iraq itself. President Barzani was invited to Washington to meet with President Obama in this regard. The meeting in January 2010 resulted in both sides issuing statements affirming the importance of a long term relationship between the United States and all of Iraq, including the Kurdistan Region. The White House release stated, 'The President

extended U.S. good offices to help Iraqis move forward in forging a broad political consensus to resolve outstanding disagreements between the Kurdistan Regional Government and the Government of Iraq, in accordance with the Iraqi constitution and working closely with the United Nations in these efforts.'

The UN had spent more than 18 months compiling a 500-page report on Iraq's disputed internal boundaries. Other than actually naming disputed areas for the first time (the constitution only mentions Kirkuk by name) the report offered only tentative suggestions. On the hot topic of Kirkuk, the report suggested four possible scenarios for consideration by the various actors – namely the KRG and Baghdad. Although most parties expect the UN Assistance Mission for Iraq, or UNAMI, to be integral in finding ways

Left:
Young children are growing up in Kurdistan today with unprecedented access to education and other opportunities. These Yezidi children will have the chance to make an important contribution to the future of their country.

Opposite:
Meeting the aspirations of the Kurdish youth and incorporating them into the political culture of the country will be crucial to building broad support for the state and its activities.

forward, this initial report seems to have met with limited success.

The issue of decision-making and representation in diverse territories, such as Kirkuk, was always going to be difficult.

Saadi Ahmed Pire, a senior figure in the PUK, reflects on the difference between proportional representation and a simplistic quota system. 'We always say that Kirkuk is a city that is located inside the borders of the Kurdistan region. It is a multi-ethnic and multi-religious city and we should respect the views and rights of all its people. Just as in the rest of Iraq it will require the majority population, the Arabs, to accept that the Kurds have legitimate national aspirations and are genuinely seeking a partnership with Iraq's Arabs, rather than a relationship based, as in the past, on subjugation.'

Since 2003, the question of Kirkuk has met with procrastination rather than decision making. In the meantime, views have hardened to the extent that the issue of Kirkuk was threatening to delay crucial national elections.

The trouble is that many Arabs simply don't believe the Kurds when they say that they want to stay in Iraq. They believe that Kurdish control of Kirkuk and its adjacent oilfields is merely the preliminary gambit to a declaration of independence. The dispute over Kirkuk is thus seen as a zero sum game. Either Kirkuk remains part of Arab Iraq, or it goes to the Kurds.

It is a view that seems to ignore the salient fact that no Kurdish leaders currently advocate an independent state, or are likely so to do in the foreseeable future. Indeed Kurdish leaders say they grow weary of repeating their loyalty to Iraq and their determination to see it work.

They point out that Kurdish blood was shed during Iraq's liberation from dictatorship. It was shed, further, in the fight against terrorism, and in keeping the peace between Shia and Sunni Arabs in Baghdad and other parts of Iraq outside of the Kurdistan Region.

At the inauguration of the new KRG administration in Erbil on October 28 2009, President Masoud Barzani made an important promise. 'We will not look away and disengage with Baghdad,' he said. 'On the contrary, we will look to Baghdad, and we will try to strengthen ourselves in Baghdad. We are key partners in the political process and the rebuilding of Iraq… Following the liberation of Iraq, we demonstrated that we are part of the political process in Iraq and we protected the unity of Iraq. We will not hesitate to build a federal, democratic and multi-party Iraq.'

Iraqi Kurds often say they dream of independence but know this is not realizable, hence their strategy of remaining part of a federal Iraq. Distributing political, economic and military power by law helps, but it does not create long-term stability. Federalism is about more than just laws. If Iraq is to stay united and thrive, it is up to the majority Arabs to convince rather than coerce the Kurds into believing that their long-term future lies within the Iraqi state.

The Kurds need also to give guarantees that they will be guided by the rule of law and submit to federal authority when required by dictates of the constitution. They will need to respect and safeguard the rights of ethnic and religious minorities that live within the areas under KRG administration.

The Kurdish issue in Iraq will not disappear by itself. Success will be the art of allowing for democracy, justice and the rule of law to take its course while minimizing resentment.

At Home

On the domestic front, the tasks of the new regional administration led by Prime Minister Barham Salih are easily identifiable, although no less tricky.

Kurds face several important issues. These include completing the unification of the KRG security and intelligence apparatus, forging ahead with reconstruction and economic development, further democratisation of the political system, fighting corruption, and ensuring transparency and accountability.

The Kurds will need to build on the advances they have set in motion since the unification of the KRG in 2006. Above all, the Kurds will need to develop their human resources. How this is accomplished will set the tone for generations to come. The mindset in the past has been one of survival, and many Kurds still think of short-term gains rather than

Above:
The relationship between Kurdistan and Turkey will depend heavily on continued effective trade and commercial relations. While there might be tensions in some areas, cross-border trade will do a lot to maintain peaceful and amicable relations between the two countries.

Following pages:
At the dawn of the twenty-first century Kurdistan is making a name for itself as one of the great success stories of the Middle East. There is every reason to believe that the banner of prosperity and development will be held aloft at the close of the century and beyond.

long-term profit and growth. History has taught them to be this way. There is also an understandable – almost genetic – distrust of power and authority. Citizens of the Region will need to learn to trust their own institutions, and the institutions must act in a way so as to earn that trust.Large amounts of money will continue to pour into the region as the economy continues to develop. It will need to be used wisely and transparently for the benefit of all the region's citizens.

Many of the issues of inefficiency and corruption that have dogged the KRG over the past few years have their roots in the rivalry between the two dominant political forces, the PUK and KDP. Internal divisions in the mid-90s, and the subsequent dual administrations within the KRG, created a tangle of competing institutional authorities and powers that has proven difficult, administratively, to unravel.

Senior Kurdish politicians have a history that is rooted in the long mountain struggle against a regime with a genocidal tendency. It has been difficult for some of them to adjust to the frequently humdrum requirements of nation building. But adjust they must, or make way for a new generation of Kurds more attuned to the needs of a globalised world and whose expectations and aspirations have amplified since 2003.

During the regional elections in summer 2009, the message of reform, embodied by a new political movement Goran (meaning Change), threatened for the first time the duopoly on power enjoyed by the KDP and PUK since the start of self-rule in 1991. Goran campaigned on an anti-corruption platform that struck a chord with Kurdistan's predominantly youthful electorate, particularly in Suleimaniah. It emerged with a significant bloc of seats in the Kurdistan national assembly.

It remains to be seen whether Goran performs its duties as an opposition responsibly, and whether Kurds are capable of disagreeing at home, yet remaining united in Baghdad on the so-called national issues such as Kirkuk, disputed territories, and decentralisation.

The elections for the parliament of the Kurdistan region in July 2009 may yet prove to be a watershed. They may prove to be a sign of the maturing of the democratic process in Kurdistan.

In his inaugural speech as Prime Minister, Mr Salih, said, 'We are committed to the implementation of the agenda of renewal and reconstruction; we want to transform our words into action.' Mr Salih continued, 'We all know that there is criticism of government performance and the methods of self-rule, since our government has not been able to fulfill all the needs and wishes of the people of Kurdistan. We hear such criticism and comments, and we will not shy away from them.'

Mr Salih said the KRG would work for all sections and interests in Kurdistan's society, from reforming the agricultural sector, the provision of social housing, to supporting civil society and providing opportunities for women and young people, as well as continuing to liberalise and boost the economy. He would, he said, be guided by the ideas of 'political freedom and public determination.'

Getting on with the Neighbours

The Kurds of Iraq live in the toughest of regional neighborhoods. Surrounded by Turkey, Iran and Syria, each with a significant Kurdish population, every move made by the KRG is and will continue to be closely scrutinized.

But the political landscape has changed markedly since 2003.

The days when the Kurds were strategically used as bargaining chips in what passed for regional diplomacy appear to be over. No longer just a humanitarian issue, they have become part of the new political reality of the Middle East.

Western diplomats in Baghdad once euphemistically referred to the semi-autonomous area only as 'northern Iraq,' for fear of upsetting Turkey. Iraq is now a federal state, and the existence of the Kurdistan Region is enshrined in the country's permanent constitution. Today there are 17 diplomatic represent-ations from various countries in Erbil, the capital of the Kurdistan region. Historically, former adversary Turkey has opened a consulate in Erbil.

Influential KRG representation offices exist in ten key cities around the world, including London, Washington, Brussels, Berlin and Paris. President Barzani has stressed the need 'to expand relations with the Region's neighbours, Arab states, and the international community in general in order to promote better understanding and enhance political and economic relations.'

Especially notable is the about face in relations with Turkey. The presence of guerrillas of the Kurdistan Workers' Party (or PKK) in the remote mountain areas straddling the Turkish-Iraq border brought accusations from Ankara that Erbil was supporting a movement regarded by Turkey, the EU and the US as a terrorist outfit. Turkish armed forces have staged regular bombardments of supposed PKK hideouts in KRG-controlled territory. With the green light from Washington in 2007 the Turkish military launched a large-scale military incursion into Iraq's northernmost regions on the pretext of battling the PKK. Many Kurds, however, thought the PKK issue merely a subtext to Ankara's real intention, which was to destabilize KRG territory. Turkey is particularly concerned about Kurdish claims to Kirkuk, which is also home to a historic Turkomen population.

KRG leaders have urged the PKK either to lay down their arms or to leave Iraq. The KRG has taken steps to cut supply lines to the rebel group, but refused to contemplate military action.

However, while tensions between Ankara and Erbil over the PKK neared crisis point, Turkish and Kurdish businessmen were quietly consolidating impressive cross-border trade and investment, building an economic platform upon which political relations could then develop. Turkish construction companies were involved in some of the KRG's major infrastructure projects, building roads, hospitals and airports. With the rising standard of living

157

in the Kurdistan Region, Turkish consumer goods found an important new market. Most importantly, perhaps, was Turkey's involvement in Kurdistan's nascent oil industry.

Turkey's political view of the KRG began to change. It was no longer viewed as an existential threat; rather as a potential partner and a reasonable political actor. At the same time, Ankara began taking steps, in some cases unprecedented initiatives, to address its own internal Kurdish population. On October 30, 2009, Turkey's Foreign Minister Professor Ahmet Davutoglu made a landmark visit to Erbil for talks with President Masoud Barzani. It was the first time a Turkish foreign minister had traveled to the Kurdistan Region of Iraq.

Following the meeting, in a joint press conference with the Turkish Foreign Minister, President Barzani described the visit as 'an important step, indeed a historic step. We know that Turkey has an important role in our development, and this relationship requires special attention. Both men spoke with optimism on a number of issues, including security, enhancement of commercial ties, and economic cooperation. Putting flesh on the improved relations, Turkey announced it would open a second border crossing into the KRG Region and open a consulate in Erbil. It was further evidence of the vital role that economic ties between the Kurds and their neighbours will play in guaranteeing future regional stability. For most Kurds, therefore, Turkish accession to the EU would be the icing on the cake.

The KRG will also need to further enhance relations with Syria and Iran, doing more business, and reassuring both Damascus and Tehran that the success of the KRG will not instigate discontent among their own Kurdish populations.

On the contrary, Iraq's Kurds believe they can be a moderate, stabilizing force in the wider region. President Barzani works tirelessly to remind the world that Iraq's Kurds are not a threat to anyone.

INDEX